Evita's KOSSIE SIKELELA

Evita's KOSSIE SIKELELA

Evita Bezuidenhout

Design,
Drawings + Dishes –
Linda Vicquery

UMUZI

'In the City of Dreams in 1992 I gave my presentation of where South Africa was going and found footprints on a sidewalk that every woman wants to fill – as well as Sophia Loren's signature on Hollywood Boulevard. Imagine my delight when she agreed to introduce this cookbook!'

Foreword

The first time I saw Evita Bezuidenhout was at her presentation in Hollywood in 1992. I immediately realised that everything she had didn't just come from eating spaghetti!

This delightful cookbook proves it – a unique collection of mainly South African recipes and some others, lovingly presented.

I heard that Evita, this most famous white woman in South Africa, passionately believes that reconciliation can happen around the dinner table. Give enemies a plate of glorious food and watch them become friends? We all agree.

Viva Evita!

Sophia Loren

SOPHIA LOREN

Sophia with a fan in Hollywood, 1992

Contents

'To eat, to love,
to sing and to
digest, in truth,
these are the four
acts in this Opera
Bouffe that we
call life and which
vanishes like the
bubbles in a bottle
of champagne.'
– Rossini

Tannie Evita's Notes

Unless otherwise stated ...

- all recipes serve 4
- use medium-sized eggs
- use full fat milk
- standard level spoon measurements are used in all recipes
- except when olive oil is indicated, use canola, peanut, sunflower or grapeseed oil.

Conversion table
1 tsp (teaspoon) = 5 ml
1 tbs (tablespoon) = 15 ml
1 cup = 250 ml

'My food guru Linda Vicquery and I have tried to interpret recipes given to us as best we could. Everything I cook tastes wonderful anyway, as I put in that extra special mysterious ingredient – passion!'

Introduction

Evita Bezuidenhout, regarded as the most famous white woman in South Africa, was born Evangelie Poggenpoel of humble Boer origins in the dusty Orange Free State town of Bethlehem on the 28th September 1935. Illegitimate, imaginative, pretty and ambitious, she dreamed of Hollywood fame and fortune, tasting stardom in such 50s Afrikaner film classics as *Boggel en die Akkedis* (Hunchback and the Lizard), *Meisie van my Drome* (Girl of my Dreams) and *Duiwelsvallei* (Devil's Valley). She married into the political Bezuidenhout dynasty and became the demure wife of NP Member of Parliament Dr JJ De V Bezuidenhout and proud mother of three: De Kock, Izan and Billie-Jeanne.

Power became her addiction. She wielded it in the boardroom, the kitchen and around the dinner table, becoming confidante to the flawed gods on the Boer Olympus and so shaping the course of history with her close, often unbelievable relationships with the grim-faced leaders of the day: Dr HF Verwoerd, BJ Vorster, PW Botha and FW de Klerk. Hand in hand with the glamorous Evita of Pretoria were the Talleyrand of Africa, Pik Botha, her ageing Romeo and constant friend, and, while watching her from afar as she watched him, Nelson R Mandela, alive today thanks to her timely interventions.

From 1981, her ten years as the South African Ambassador in the independent black homeland republic of Bapetikosweti left an indelible mark on the blueprint of change, and today her recipe for bobotie is internationally regarded as the basis for reconciliation. *Sit down, eat and talk* has been her slogan, and trouble spots in the world owe their future to her kitchen skills.

As the former barefoot-meisie from Bethlehem majestically sailed into the stormy seas of her marriage and maturity, dazzling friend and foe alike with her Calvinist authority and dreaded lack of irony, like any other educated brainwashed white South African, she constantly passed by the terrible aftermath of the apartheid system she had helped to spawn, and having seen, looked away at her smiling reflection in the family silver. When in 1994, democracy swallowed her homeland and her job, and when Nelson Mandela stood at the Union Buildings in Pretoria and said those immortal words: *Never. Never. Never again whites only!*, Evita sat next to him with a big smile and applauded.

She went into his kitchen and cooked for him and the hundreds of politicians who flocked to Pretoria to meet the most famous man in the world and to have their picture taken with Madiba, so that everyone would think they were also upholders of democracy and human rights. Democrats like Muammar Gaddafi,

Fidel Castro, Yasser Arafat, Robert Mugabe, Tony Blair and the Spice Girls all came to Pretoria and sampled Evita's cooking.

She then went to Parliament to join the kitchen there and help the ANC Government come to terms with African cuisine after a lifetime in exile. She served putupap with everything: putupap with bread-and-butter pudding, putupap with sushi, putupap with the Atkins Diet.

Evita Bezuidenhout was presented with the Living Legacy Award 2000 in San Diego, USA. This same award has been given to legends that include Hillary Rodham Clinton, Bette Davis, Princess Diana and Margaret Thatcher. Today Evita divides her time between the family home in Laagerfontein where her husband Oom Hasie lives, and the West Coast village of Darling where her mother Ouma Ossewania Kakebenia resides.

Now in her 70s, this glamorous eternal flame of Boere chutzpah holds court at the former Darling Station, now famous as *Evita se Perron*, where she dazzles a visiting world in awe, while also bravely following in the slipstream of Jacob Zuma's presidential jet to make sure that kos is on his tafel. As one of the few Afrikaner icons who did not lose their head on the tumbrels of democracy, Gogo Evita is grandmother to her three black treasures: Winnie-Jeanne, Nelson-Ignatius, and La Toya-Ossewania. She embraced the new democracy with an alarming passion, underlining her commitment to a nonracial future by her support that cuts across party lines. She may still stand for the Presidency of South Africa in a future general election.

Chicken Soup & Stock

'Before we start, I simply must share the magic of all good cooking. Golda Meir gave me her secret weapon: her very own recipe for "Golden Broth" as she called it. There are many variations, for example boiling a whole chicken, adding bay leaves, fennel seed, a bunch of thyme or orange peel, a pinch of saffron or turmeric, a diced tomato and so on, but here is her classic recipe for "Jewish penicillin".'

Roast a good farm chicken. The roasted bones add taste and colour to the soup. Put 2 litres of water into a large stock pot. Add the chicken carcass, keeping the meat to use in another dish. Add the giblets, onions, leek, turnip and carrots, all cut into fat chunks; also add the celery, salt, parsley stalks and peppercorns.

Bring to the boil; then simmer gently over low heat for about an hour and a half. Strain the soup into a bowl and allow to cool. Chill and remove the fat once it has floated to the top. *Voilá!* You have chicken soup!

This soup or stock can be used as the basis for most soups and sauces, and can also be added to pasta and used to cook risotto. Its wonderful flavour adds richness all round. It can be kept in the fridge for up to three days. Alternatively, freeze in small batches for future use.

1 farm chicken with giblets
2 medium onions, unpeeled
1 leek
1 turnip, halved
2 carrots
2 celery stalks with leaves
8 peppercorns
parsley stalks

Soups

Waterblommetjie soup

1 onion
500 g waterblommetjies
3 cups chicken stock
lemon juice
1 cup cream
a dash of sherry

In a large pot, slowly sauté chopped onion in a little oil until transparent. Wash and rinse waterblommetjies thoroughly, cut off the stems and place in the pot with the onions Add the chicken stock and simmer gently until they are soft – about 15 minutes or so. Add the lemon juice, salt and pepper. Stir. Liquidise using a hand blender, leaving the soup a little chunky. Lastly, add the cream and a dash of sherry to taste.

Courgette soup

10 firm small courgettes
1 leek
1 clove of garlic
1 potato
3 cups chicken stock
1 cup crème fraîche
1 tsp lemon juice and zest
fresh basil

Cut courgettes and leek into rounds. Use white and green parts of leek. Heat 1 tbs oil in a large pot, add the vegetables and garlic and sauté gently for 3 minutes. Add the chopped potato and chicken stock and simmer for 20 minutes. Mix in the crème fraîche, lemon zest and juice and a handful of basil leaves. Taste and season. This soup can be served hot, at room temperature or is delicious cold. Just before serving, sprinkle each bowl with a little Parmesan cheese and chopped chives.

Tomato & shrimp soup

1 medium onion
1 tbs butter
2 cloves of garlic
4 tomatoes (or 1 can)
1 tsp sugar
1 cup shrimps
½ cup white wine
a pinch of cayenne pepper
a dash of brandy
1 cup cream

Chop onion finely and sauté gently in 1 tbs oil and butter until transparent, adding a little chopped garlic at the end. In another pot, cook roughly chopped tomatoes (or use canned) and add sugar. Set aside. Combine cooked, shelled shrimps with onion in the pan and add the white wine. Add this to the pot containing tomatoes. Stir well and add a pinch of cayenne pepper and a dash of brandy. Stir and simmer slowly for a few minutes before adding the cream to turn it a lovely pink colour.

Pea & bacon soup

Soak the peas in water for an hour. Drain and put into a large pot with chicken stock, onion, carrot, garlic, bay leaf and winter savoury. Bring to the boil and simmer for an hour. In the meantime, fry bacon until crispy, in a small pan. Remove. Fry cubed bread in the same pan to brown. Set aside on kitchen paper. Remove herbs from soup. Using a hand blender, blend the soup in the pot. Season to taste. To serve, spoon soup into individual bowls and sprinkle bacon pieces and a few croutons on top.

Variation: For a very substantial meal, add cooked, smoky sausages cut into rounds, instead of the bacon, and sprinkle with lots of chopped parsley.

500 g split peas
1,5 *l* chicken stock
  (or use 2 stock cubes)
1 onion, chopped
1 carrot, chopped
2 cloves of garlic
bay leaf, winter savoury
100 g bacon
2 slices bread, cubed

Pumpkin soup

Peel and deseed the pumpkin and apple and cut into small chunks. Melt butter in a large pot. Add pumpkin, apple, orange peel and cumin and stir for 3 minutes. Add a cup of water and cook over low heat for 20 minutes. Purée the pulp with a hand blender. Add chicken stock. Bring to the boil. Simmer for 5 minutes. Season and stir in cream. Add a dash or two of sherry. Sprinkle with chopped parsley and black pepper. Serve with a swirl of cream.

750 g pumpkin
1 apple
2 tbs butter
a strip of orange peel
1 tsp ground cumin
3 cups chicken stock
½ cup cream
sherry
parsley

Vegetables

'There is nothing like freshly picked garden peas. Even though it is a very easy plant to grow, only vegetable gardeners can enjoy this luxury nowadays. Treat your guests to a glass of white wine and let them pod the peas themselves for a delicious springtime hors d'oeuvre. Mangetout or snow peas can be steamed or stirfried and eaten pod and all. Frozen peas – your only alternative – can be prepared as shown below.'

French-style peas

6 outer lettuce leaves
6 spring onions
2 cups frozen peas
1 tbs butter

Coarsely shred the lettuce and place in a heavy pot with ½ cup of water. Cut up the spring onions and add to the lettuce. Put the peas on top of this and then add the butter. Cover tightly and slowly bring to the boil. Lower the heat and cook for 5 minutes. Mix together and serve at once, adding salt and pepper to taste. Mangetout can also be cooked in this style – just add bacon for flavour.

Baby spinach

500 g baby spinach leaves
dill
olive oil
feta cheese

Wash spinach and cook for 5 minutes. Transfer to a pan, heat and wait for moisture to evaporate. Sprinkle in dill and mix. Drizzle olive oil on top, and add salt and pepper to taste. Crumble a few chunks of feta cheese on top.

Or, instead of olive oil, you could pour 1 cup of fresh cream over the spinach and chop up 2 hard-boiled eggs. Combine the eggs with the spinach and cream, transfer to an ovenproof dish and bake for 10 minutes at 180°C.

Waterblommetjies

Waterblommetjies are gathered in Western Cape dams and rivers during springtime. Rinse thoroughly before cooking. Bredie is the most traditional way of preparing waterblommetjies, slowly cooked with lamb, onions and potatoes. However, these aromatic little blommetjies can be appreciated in other dishes too. The taste is reminiscent of artichokes, as Sophia remarked when I once treated her to waterblommetjie pasta.

Waterblommetjie pasta

Steam the well-rinsed waterblommetjies until cooked, but not too soft. Cook the penne in a large pot of salted boiling water, stirring regularly. Mix the cream and Parmesan in a bowl. Drain penne as soon as al dente, keeping 1 cup of pasta water aside to dilute the sauce if necessary. Put the pasta in a large pan, add waterblommetjies, pour the cream mixture over these and toss gently to heat through. Serve straight from the pan with lots of black pepper and extra Parmesan to sprinkle over once everybody is seated.

400 g waterblommetjies
400 g penne
1 cup cream
1 cup grated Parmesan
   cheese

Mousse

Crush cooked waterblommetjies into a rough purée – or chop up, using knife and fork. Add cream cheese and mix together with lemon juice and cream. Season with sea salt and black pepper. A drop or 3 of Tabasco or a pinch of tarragon can be added. Serve with crackers or herb toasts as a starter.

1 cup cooked
   waterblommetjies
1 cup smooth cream cheese
1 tsp lemon juice
2 tbs cream

Parmesan toasts

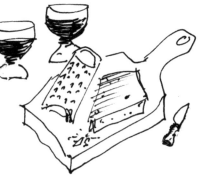

Slice a day-old French loaf and place the slices on a baking sheet. Drizzle a little olive oil over the slices. Sprinkle grated Parmesan cheese on top. Place under hot grill for 2 minutes. Watch them carefully to make sure that they don't burn. Serve with soup, or as a snack with drinks.

Asparagus omelette

6 eggs
1 tbs cream
1 tbs butter
300 g fresh asparagus tips,
or 1 tin, drained

Lightly beat the eggs in a bowl with cream, salt and pepper. Heat butter and oil in a large frying pan. Sauté the asparagus tips for about 5 minutes, tossing now and then. Pour the egg mixture over the hot asparagus. Draw the edges to the centre as soon as the omelette begins to set. Fold it over in the pan, and then slide onto a serving dish. Cut into four pieces. Garnished with chervil and grated Parmesan, this makes a very good starter or a light lunch for two.

Easy cauliflower cheese

1 cauliflower
1 cup cream
Gruyère cheese
nutmeg

Separate the florets. Drop into boiling water for 3 minutes or so – they must be firm, not soft. Drain. Put into a shallow ovenproof gratin dish. Pour cream over to cover. Scatter grated Gruyère, cheddar or Parmesan cheese on top, and then a little grated nutmeg. Bake at 180°C for 10 minutes until the cheese has melted and browned.

Sweet & sour pearl onions

500 g pearl onions
3 tbs red wine vinegar
1 tbs sugar
2 tbs raisins, currants or sultanas

Peel the onions (one way of doing this is to plunge them into boiling water until the skins come off easily). Sauté in oil on low heat, swirling them around in the pan to brown them thoroughly. Add vinegar, sugar and raisins and cook gently until soft, adding a little water if necessary. Season.

Variation: For caramelised onions, sauté the pearl onions slowly in oil. Add 1 tbs grated ginger, 1 tbs brown sugar and 2 tbs balsamic vinegar and keep sautéing gently until soft, adding a little water to moisten if necessary. Sultanas can be added. Delicious served with all roasts.

Leeks

'Baby leeks in spring and mature leeks in winter – I just love leeks! – are delicious with potatoes. The classic soup vichyssoise is always a treat, served either hot or cold. Slowly sauté 2 chopped leeks in a little butter. Add 4 cups of chicken stock and diced potatoes. Simmer until potatoes are soft. Blend, adding cream, salt and pepper.'

Leeks on toast

Sauté chopped leeks – the white part only – in a little butter and oil. Cook until soft, adding water (or stock) if necessary. Also add a dash of cream, and salt and pepper. Spoon onto toast – a tasty snack instead of baked beans on toast and a different starter to replace the equally delicious mushrooms on toast.

Baked leeks

My old friend Mary McNeill, a direct descendant of the 1820 Settlers, gave me this recipe – an old Scottish classic, which her family have been cooking ever since they arrived here ...

Boil the potatoes, and sauté the leeks in a little stock until soft. Mash the potatoes and combine with the leeks in the pot. Add the cream, chives, salt and pepper, and mix well. Transfer to an ovenproof dish, grate cheese on top and bake in the oven for 10 to 15 minutes at 180°C, or until top is golden.

2 potatoes
2 leeks, white part only
stock
2 tbs cream
1 tbs chopped chives
cheddar cheese

Red cabbage

Heat oil in heavy-based pot. Add the bacon and brown lightly. Add the onion and stir for a few minutes. Add the shredded cabbage, apples, wine and salt. Simmer gently for about 40 minutes, or until cabbage is cooked. Grind black pepper over the entire dish.

diced streaky bacon
1 onion, chopped
1 medium red cabbage
2 apples, peeled, cored and
  diced
½ cup red wine

Apéritif Snacks

'For snacks, allow four to five pieces per person and for a cocktail party lasting 2 hours, four to five pieces per person for the first hour and four pieces per hour thereafter. Put out bowls of olives and almonds, dips and crackers and some good sliced ham and salami. Arrange on a platter with pickled cucumbers. Quails' eggs always add glamour. For 20 people, allow ten bottles of wine and two types of cocktails. Champagne cocktails or dry martinis are great to get the ball rolling ... or for having a ball!'

Bruschetta

Toast a few slices of good bread. Top with diced tomato, garlic, basil and olive oil, or with chopped sautéed mushrooms with cream and chives.

Baby potato sandwich

Boil a few baby potatoes. Cool. Slice in half. Put an anchovy between slices and seal with a toothpick.

Stuffed eggs

Hard-boil eggs. Halve them and remove yolks. Mash and combine with tinned tuna, and use to refill egg halves.

Cheese toasts

Slice a baguette. Drizzle with olive oil. Top with cheese, then tomato. Sprinkle with thyme and a little more olive oil, and grill until brown.

Chicken balls

Recipe (p. 79).
Make mini kebabs by spiking three chicken balls on a skewer and dip in tomato sauce.

Bobotie squares

Recipe (p. 75). Cut into small squares and spike with a toothpick to serve.

Zucchini blinis

Grate courgettes; place on kitchen paper to drain off water. Beat 2 eggs. Add grated courgettes, salt and pepper. Spoon into blini pan. Cook both sides. Serve with a dollop of sour cream on top. Sprinkle with chopped chives.

Hot cashew nuts

Heat 1 tbs oil in a pan. Add 1 tsp curry powder, a good pinch of peri-peri and salt. Sauté the nuts until golden and well-coated with oil. Drain on kitchen paper.

Slimming Canapes

'Having people around for an apéritif is a relaxing way to entertain those whom you have recently met, or if you don't want to cook a full-on dinner. It is a great way to catch up with old friends as nowadays everyone seems too busy. Create light, slimming appetisers, alternating colours, textures and tastes. Try out new combinations, giving free rein to your imagination.'

Stuffed tomatoes

Cut cherry tomatoes in half and spoon out the pulp. Mix drained tinned tuna with low-fat cream cheese and fill tomato halves. Sprinkle with black pepper.

Chicken satays

Cut chicken breasts into strips. Thread onto a skewer. Marinate in lemon juice, soy sauce, grated ginger, chilli and garlic for an hour. Place under a hot grill for 3 to 4 minutes on each side.

Crudités

Cut up various raw vegetables. Place on a plate with a dip of yoghurt and chopped chilli. Use cauliflower and broccoli florets, carrots cut into sticks, mushrooms (whole or halved), celery stalks, and red and yellow pepper strips.

Cucumber rounds

Slice a cucumber thickly. Top with small pieces of smoked salmon and a little horseradish sauce.

Wrapped asparagus

Wrap thin slices of ham around small white tinned asparagus.

Tomato & mozzarella

Spike cherry tomatoes and mozzarella balls together using toothpicks.
   Variation: Add rolled-up slices of Parma ham.

Prawn kebabs

Alternate cooked prawns and triangles of red pepper on a small skewer.

Elmie Erasmus 2000

Salad Sensations

'When entertaining in summer, I like to compose substantial salads for a main course. Create your own using fresh, crunchy, unusual and interesting combinations. Make them colourful and appealing to the eye. Grilled or roasted vegetables, like red and yellow peppers, courgettes, fennel, butternut, sweet potato and aubergine, served cold, make delicious salad meals. Their flavours are enhanced by grilling and roasting.'

Pomegranate salad

1 English cucumber, peeled and seeded
seeds of 1 pomegranate
1 yellow sweet pepper
a bunch of fresh coriander
1 roll goat's cheese, sliced
2 tbs pomegranate juice
2 tbs balsamic vinegar
1 tbs olive oil

Cut cucumber into small chunks. Place in a bowl with pomegranate seeds, sliced yellow pepper and a handful or two of fresh coriander. Combine with dressing of pomegranate juice, balsamic vinegar and olive oil, salt and pepper. Transfer to a serving platter and arrange sliced goat's cheese on top.

Roast sweet potato & couscous

Toss sweet potato wedges in a little oil and place in a baking dish. Bake in preheated 200°C oven for 20 minutes until soft and slightly charred around the edges. Set aside. Bring a cup of salted water to the boil. Turn off heat and add the cup of couscous. Cover and leave for 5 minutes to swell. Add a tablespoon of olive oil and stir with a fork to separate the grains. Toss couscous, sweet potato and spring onions together in a bowl. Make the dressing, combining yoghurt, cumin, garlic and chilli. Arrange rocket on a serving platter, then top with sweet potato and couscous. Pour over dressing and sprinkle with chopped peanuts.

4 medium sweet potatoes,
   cut into wedges
1 cup water
1 cup couscous
4 spring onions, chopped
1 cup yoghurt
1 tsp ground cumin
1 clove of garlic, crushed
chilli, 200 g rocket leaves
2 tsp peanuts

Aubergine & chickpeas

Heat oil in a heavy-based frying pan. Add garlic, coriander, cumin and fennel seeds and cook quickly for a minute. Add the aubergines. Stir for a few minutes to brown. Add the chickpeas and cook for 3 or 4 minutes until heated through. Add a dash of water if necessary. Add parsley, sea salt and extra chopped garlic and stir to mix well. Remove from heat. Place mixed salad leaves on a serving plate. Top with aubergine and chickpea mix. Serve with tzatziki and lots of crusty bread.

3 cloves of garlic, chopped
2 tsp ground coriander
1 tsp ground cumin
1 tsp fennel seeds
2 aubergines, chopped
   into chunks
2 cups tinned chickpeas
2 tbs parsley
mixed salad leaves

Courgette & tomato salad

Cut courgettes lengthwise. Place in roasting dish. Drizzle over olive oil and grill one side only, until brown. Transfer to a serving dish. Layer courgette and tomato slices, alternating the layers. Scatter black olives and fresh basil leaves. Drizzle olive oil, salt and pepper – and crumbled feta cheese, if you wish.

4 medium courgettes
olive oil
2 large ripe tomatoes
black olives
fresh basil

Butternut & pasta salad

1 medium butternut
300 g bowtie pasta
feta cheese
pumpkin seeds

Peel and deseed butternut. Cut into small cubes. Place in an overproof dish and drizzle over a little oil. Toss, using your hands, to coat well. Bake in a 220°C oven for 30 minutes or until cooked and browned around the edges. Cook bowtie pasta until al dente. Drain. Transfer butternut cubes and pasta to a serving bowl. Add chunks of feta cheese, scatter a handful of pumpkin seeds. Drizzle over oil, salt and pepper, and a sprinkling of chopped, fresh chilli if you like it hot.

Fennel & caper salad

2 large fennel bulbs
2 tbs olive oil
2 tbs capers
parsley
2 hard-boiled eggs
4 anchovies

Cut off green stalks and remove outer sheaths of fennel (keep for soup). Cut in half, and then into thin slices. Sauté in a little olive oil, adding a dash of water now and then to keep moist. Cook for about 8 minutes – transfer to a salad bowl and toss with capers, parsley and olive oil. Decorate with quartered boiled eggs and anchovies and lots of black pepper.

Aubergine & red peppers

2 aubergines
olive oil
2 red peppers
1 tbs pine nuts
1 tbs capers
1 tbs garlic and parsley,
chopped
Parmesan shavings

Cut aubergines lengthwise. Drizzle olive oil over them and place them under a hot grill for 8 minutes, both sides, until brown. Cut red peppers in half, remove seeds and place in a roasting dish under a hot grill until skin is black and blistered. Remove, place in a bowl and cover with clingwrap until cool enough to handle. The skin will peel away easily as it steams under the cover. Cut aubergines and peppers into long strips. Arrange on a serving platter, alternating the colours. Scatter pine nuts, capers, a mixture of chopped garlic and parsley over this, as well as salt, pepper and Parmesan shavings.

Potato & feta salad

Boil potatoes in skins until tender. Do not overcook. Drain and cool. Peel potatoes and place in a salad bowl. Keep whole if small, if not, cut potatoes in half. Add chopped spring onions, capers, olives, feta and herbs and mix very gently. Make the vinaigrette. In a small bowl, stir mustard together with salt and vinegar. Then add the oil, stirring. Pour this over the salad while potatoes are still warm.

Variations: Instead of the capers and olives, add 150 g cooked green beans chopped into small pieces, and 100 g fried streaky bacon pieces.

Or add 2 chopped tomatoes, 2 hard-boiled eggs and a handful of chopped chives.

You could also add a tin of tuna, drained and flaked. Omit the feta cheese, but add the capers and olives, and 2 chopped hard-boiled eggs and extra spring onions.

300 g small new potatoes
4 spring onions
1 tbs capers
10 black olives
100 g feta cheese, cubed
2 tbs chopped parsley
2 tbs chopped mint
1 tsp Dijon mustard
1 tsp red wine vinegar
3 tbs olive oil

Cape Malay Inspirations

'We have much for which to thank the Cape Malays. They are very artful cooks. Their culinary tradition has played a huge role in blending Eastern and Western styles of cooking, and in so doing they have defined our country's cuisine in terms of that which we have eventually proudly come to call traditional South African food. I just love bredies, biryanis, curries, various pies, gesmoorde chicken, sosaties, and so on. Here are a few simple recipes inspired by these creative Malay cooks for you to enjoy as your daily fare if you wish, or to entertain those expats when they return, hungry and homesick for these Cape flavours and colours.'

Basis for bredies & stews

Braising is a very old form of cooking, which we have inherited from the East. The Cape Malays brought this method with them. It is a combination of sautéing in a little oil or fat, then continuing to cook in very little liquid, so that the food cooks in its own juices. The dish can either continue to simmer in a pot on top of the stove, or can be transferred to an ovenproof dish after braising and then placed in the oven to continue cooking.

Braise cubed meat in a little oil, or chicken or duck fat. Add chopped onions and seasoning of your choice – bay leaf, peppercorns, thyme, juniper berries, etc., or cumin, chilli, ginger, garlic, cinnamon, etc. and cover with stock, water or wine (not for your Halaal friends!) and simmer. Vegetables can be added halfway through cooking, depending on the vegetable.

24

Green bean bredie

Gently brown lamb knuckles in oil in a heavy-bottomed pot. Add the chopped onions, garlic, chilli and winter savoury. Stir and cook for a while, adding a little water now and then to keep moist and to infuse flavours. Add ½ cup beef stock and cook for an hour. Add the green beans, chopped in half, and the potato chunks. Cook for a further ½ hour, or until meat is soft. If the bredie has too much liquid, allow it to evaporate by taking the lid off the pot for the last 5 minutes of cooking time. A little grated nutmeg enhances this dish.

Serve with plain white rice.

800 g lamb knuckles
2 onions
300 g green beans
2 cloves of garlic
chilli, chopped
2 medium potatoes
1 cup beef stock
a sprig of winter savoury
grated nutmeg

Cumin chicken with sweet potatoes

Brown the chicken thighs in chicken or duck fat, or oil, skin side down first. Remove from the pan. Sauté the sliced onions, adding cinnamon, cumin, garlic and salt. Stir and simmer slowly until the onions are transparent. Add a little water to keep moist. Add red grape vinegar and quince jam (or sugar) and stir into the onion sauce.

Return the chicken to the pan and simmer gently for 20 minutes. Add the chunks of sweet potato and cook for a further 20 minutes until soft and chicken is cooked through. Sprinkle over chopped parsley and lots of black pepper 5 minutes before serving with basmati rice.

4 chicken thighs and legs
2 large onions
cinnamon stick
1½ tsp ground cumin
2 cloves of garlic, chopped
1 tbs red grape vinegar
1 tbs quince jam
   (or 1 tbs brown sugar)
2 sweet potatoes
parsley

Beef with pearl onions

Braise meat cubes slowly in oil in a heavy-bottomed pot. Add garlic, cumin, allspice berries, cinnamon and orange peel. Stir to mix, then add wine (or water if Halaal). Cook for a few minutes to evaporate, then add tomato purée, sugar and salt. Cover and simmer for an hour. Add the pickling onions and cook very gently for another 30 minutes, until meat is tender and onions soft, but not disintegrating. Add a little hot water now and then if casserole seems dry. Serve with yellow rice (p. 78) or mashed potatoes.

1 kg stewing steak
3 cloves of garlic, chopped
1 tsp ground cumin
3 allspice berries
1 cinnamon stick
1 strip orange peel
1 cup red wine
tomato purée – 1 tbs in
   2 cups water
1 tsp brown sugar
500 g pickling onions

Lamb with chickpeas

600 g lamb shoulder, cubed
1 large onion
1 stick ginger, grated
2 cloves of garlic, chopped
1 tin whole tomatoes, roughly chopped
1 tsp sugar
1 red pepper, chopped
1 strip orange peel
1 red chilli
2 cups chickpeas (tinned)

Sauté lamb cubes in oil until brown. Remove to a bowl. Sauté chopped onion until transparent. Add the ginger, garlic, tomatoes, sugar, red pepper, orange peel and chilli. Cook for 10 minutes, then return lamb to the pan and simmer for 20 minutes. Add the drained chickpeas, cover and simmer for 20 minutes, until lamb is tender. Stir now and then. Add a little water if necessary to keep moist and saucy. Add the salt at the end. Serve with basmati rice, or couscous recipe (p. 73).

Evita's pilaf

'The first time I tasted Gadidja's biryani, I thought I had died and gone to heaven. It is a very time-consuming dish to make, but well worth it – but I nevertheless came up with this quick pilaf instead.'

Even when I'm cooking for four people only, I use an extra cup of rice, so that I can enjoy the leftovers the next day. Sauté chopped onion in a heavy-bottomed pot and a little oil for a minute. Add the rice, crushed cardamom and cinnamon stick and stir for a minute to coat rice with oil. Add the water, cover and bring to the boil. Lower heat and simmer until water has evaporated.

Turn off heat and cover with clean tea cloth to absorb steam for about 10 minutes. Spoon out rice gently and transfer to a bowl and scatter with lots of pumpkin seeds, chopped garlic and parsley.

I enjoy eating this with garlic yoghurt.

The pilaf is better the next day. Use the leftovers. Gently sauté a chopped onion in a wok until transparent, adding fennel seeds, cumin and chopped green chilli. Add the rice and stir well. Add pumpkin seeds and any other seeds or nuts you fancy. Add chopped garlic, parsley and 4 spring onions and mix. You can add stir-fried chicken strips to the rice and top with a few halved hard-boiled eggs and fresh coriander to make a most satisfying dish.

1 onion, chopped
2 cups basmati rice
5 cardamom pods
1 cinnamon stick
5 cups water
pumpkin seeds
garlic
parsley

Chicken kebabs

Soak the kebab sticks in water. Cut the flesh off the thighs, and remove the skin. Put in a bowl to marinate with soy sauce, olive oil, spring onions cut into 4 mm long chunks, grated ginger and cumin, for 2 hours. Wash apricots, halve, remove pips. Drain chicken and thread onto sticks, alternating with apricots and spring onion. Braai for 5 minutes or put under the grill for 8 minutes, or cook in a large pan for 10 minutes. Dried apricots can also be used and are equally delicious. Soak in tepid water for 2 hours before using.

kebab sticks
6 chicken thighs
4 tbs soy sauce
2 tbs olive oil
8 spring onions
1 tbs grated ginger
1 tsp ground cumin
8 firm apricots

Smoorsnoek

500 g fresh or smoked snoek
2 onions, sliced
1 green chilli
4 potatoes
1 clove of garlic, chopped

If you're using fresh snoek, pan-fry slowly in a little oil until cooked. Remove from pan. In the same pan, slowly sauté the onions until transparent. Add chopped green chilli and potato cut into small cubes. Flake the snoek, removing all bones, and put into pan once potatoes are cooked. Add some chopped garlic. Stir together and serve with rice, atjar and a side salad such as tomato and onions.

Fish rissoles

500 g hake
2 slices white bread
5 spring onions, finely chopped
1 tsp crushed garlic
2 tsp ground cumin
1 tsp dried chillies
1 cup chopped fresh parsley
1 egg
flour

Mince the fresh hake, or poach it in a little water. Flake the fish. Soak the bread in water for 10 minutes. Squeeze out the water with your hands. Add to the fish with chopped spring onions, garlic, cumin, chillies, parsley, salt, pepper and egg, and mix well to bind. Shape into patties and dust lightly with flour. Shallow-fry in a nonstick pan over medium heat for 3 or 4 minutes until golden brown on both sides.

Make large patties to serve as a lunch dish with rice and some sambals, or smaller ones to serve as a snack to take on picnics.

Fish curry

2 onions
2 cloves of garlic
curry leaves
2 tomatoes
1 tsp fish masala
1 tsp ground cumin
1 tsp ground coriander
1 tsp turmeric
600 g kabeljou or kingklip
1 green pepper
fresh coriander

Finely chop the onions and sauté slowly in oil until transparent. Add crushed garlic and a few curry leaves. Add chopped tomatoes (fresh, but not overripe). Add masala, cumin, coriander and turmeric. Cook until tomatoes are soft and sauce has thickened. Add the fish pieces (in cubes or strips). Add green pepper, cut into strips. Cook until the fish is done – about 10 minutes. Turn off the heat. Add a good handful of fresh coriander leaves and set aside for about 5 minutes before serving with rice and sambals. (For a hot curry, add 1 chopped fresh green chilli, including seeds, to the onions at the beginning.)

Chilli bites

Sift both flours into a large mixing bowl. Add the chopped onion, cumin, chilli powder, turmeric, fennel, salt, coriander and spinach (you can also use the firm outer leaves of a lettuce) and mix with enough water to make a thick batter. Just before frying, stir in the baking powder. Heat sunflower oil in a wok or a deep frying pan and drop in teaspoons of batter. Fry on both sides until golden brown. Drain on kitchen paper. I serve these with garlic yoghurt!

1 cup pea flour
2 tbs self-raising flour
1 onion, finely chopped
1 tsp ground cumin
1 tsp turmeric
2 tsp chilli powder
1 tsp ground fennel seeds
a handful of chopped fresh
  coriander
a handful of shredded
  spinach
1 tsp baking powder

Walnut balls

Crush walnuts coarsely using a mortar and pestle or a food processor. Put in a bowl and add the sugar, egg and cinnamon. Mix to form a firm paste. Roll into small balls, using your hands, which you should oil to prevent the dough sticking.

Place on oiled greaseproof paper on a baking tray – not too close together, as they will expand. Bake at 180°C for 25 minutes.

2 cups walnuts
½ cup sugar
1 egg
1 tsp ground cinnamon

Pampoenkoekies

In a large bowl, combine pumpkin and egg. Sift in the flour, baking powder and a good pinch of salt. Heat peanut oil in a deep frying pan and drop in tablespoons of the mixture. Fry fritters for about 4 minutes both sides, until golden. Drain on kitchen paper. Serve hot, sprinkled with cinnamon sugar (1 tsp ground cinnamon mixed well with 4 tbs granulated sugar).

2 cups pumpkin, cooked,
  drained and mashed
1 large egg, beaten
2 tbs cake flour
1 tsp baking powder
cinnamon sugar

Halaal Dinner

'When entertaining Muslim friends, it is important and polite to respect their dietary rules. Always buy Halaal meat and poultry. "Oh ye who believe, eat of the good things with which we have supplied you and give thanks if ye are His worshippers." No pork, no blood, no birds that seize prey with their talons. Alcohol, wine and beer are also forbidden. How fortunate we are to have the Cape Malays in our community, as they have given us so many wonderful dishes, like bredies, curries, biryanis, preserves, atjars, tameletjies, kolwyntjies, bollas, etc. My friend Gadidja, who lives in the Bo-Kaap, has taught me so much about traditional Malay cuisine.'

Pickled fish

Dip fish fillets in seasoned flour and fry in sunflower oil until cooked – about 5 minutes each side. Remove and arrange in a deep dish. For the curry sauce, sauté the onions slowly in oil for a minute or two. Add the chillies and the rest of the spices. Stir, add the vinegar, water and sugar and bring to the boil. Turn down heat and simmer for 10 minutes. Season. Pour this sauce to cover the fish. When cool, refrigerate for a day or two to allow flavours to develop. Serve cold.

800 g firm fish fillets
flour
2 large onions, thinly sliced
2 green chillies, chopped
2 cloves of garlic, chopped
1 tsp grated ginger
2 tsp turmeric
2 bay leaves
½ cup white grape vinegar
½ cup water
2 tsp sugar

Pumpkin bredie

Peel and cut pumpkin into large pieces. Sauté onion in oil in a large, heavy-based pot until transparent. Cut lamb into small chunks and place on top of onions. Add chopped chilli and ginger, cinnamon stick, salt and a little water if necessary. Cook for half an hour, then add pumpkin pieces and cook for a further half hour, covered, until soft. Serve with rice and sambals or grated quince.

500 g pumpkin or butternut
1 onion, sliced
1 kg shoulder of lamb
1 chilli
1 tbs grated ginger
1 cinnamon stick

Chicken curry

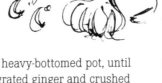

Slice onions and sauté slowly in a heavy-bottomed pot, until transparent. Add chicken pieces, grated ginger and crushed garlic, cardamom, cinnamon, cumin, coriander and thinly sliced tomatoes, and let this simmer for 20 minutes or so. Add the curry powder and turmeric, and a cup of water. Stir and leave to cook for another 15 minutes. Add the chopped potatoes and simmer over low heat for a further 30 minutes until curry aromas waft through the kitchen. Serve with rice and sambals.

2 onions
1.5 kg chicken pieces
1 tbs grated ginger
1 tbs crushed garlic
5 cardamom seeds
1 cinnamon stick
1 tsp ground cumin
1 tsp ground coriander
2 tomatoes
1 tbs curry powder
1 tsp turmeric
2 potatoes

Orange ambrosia

Peel oranges and cut into thin rounds. Arrange in layers in a glass bowl, sprinkling each layer generously with sugar and coconut. When bowl is full, pour the orange juice over. Chill until ready to serve. Decorate with fresh mint.

6 lovely oranges
½ cup sugar
1½ cups grated coconut
1 cup orange juice

Karoo Lamb

'This is a dish I've eaten with my friend Johannatjie, who has a wonderful vegetable garden just outside Calitzdorp, so the baby veggies are deliciously sweet and fresh. There is nothing like Karoo lamb and this is the simplest and easiest way to prepare it. Sometimes I serve this to the President for dinner, as he likes to sample our wonderful produce from around the country.'

Lamb with baby vegetables

baby vegetables
turnips, carrots
courgettes, mangetout
chicken stock
4 cloves of garlic
spring onions
2 racks of lamb
rosemary
potato purée

Rinse and clean all the vegetables and place in an ovenproof dish. Drizzle with oil, season, add a little chicken stock, whole cloves of garlic and spring onions. Cook in oven at 200°C for 40 minutes. Halfway through, put in racks of lamb with rosemary and cook for 20 minutes, if you prefer the meat pink. If not, cook for another 10 minutes. Arrange the vegetables on a serving platter, slice the rack into cutlets and place on top. Transport to the table and serve at once, with potato purée.

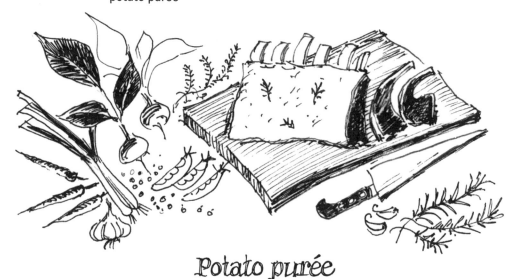

Potato purée

500 g floury potatoes
1 tbs butter
3 tbs full cream milk
2 tbs crème fraîche

Peel and cut potatoes into chunks. Boil in salted water until cooked. Drain. Put in a bowl and mash, using a fork. Add butter, milk and crème fraîche, mixing with a wooden spoon. Season with salt and pepper.

Beans fit for a queen

'Heerenbone – those wonderful beans only found in the Sandveld, also known as goewerneursboontjies – have a special place in royal circles. To this very day a bag of heerenbone is sent to the Queen of England once a year – a tradition which began more than a century ago. I usually find them in Velddrif and barter a bag with Johannatjie for half a Karoo lamb.'

Heerenbone

Soak beans overnight. Drain. Put beans in a large pot with lots of water. Add 1 star anise (to prevent flatulence). Bring to boil and cook for about an hour, bubbling gently, or until beans are soft, but not falling apart. Drain beans. Heerenbone are so delicious that they can be eaten on their own, with olive oil, salt and pepper. I sometimes sprinkle cumin over, and a squeeze of lemon.

...with onions

Sauté sliced onions very slowly in oil until transparent. Add the cooked beans, chopped garlic and parsley and a splash of red wine vinegar. This brings out the flavour. Drizzle extra olive oil over, and season to taste. Serve lamb cutlets on a bed of beans with garlic yoghurt on the side.

Lamb casserole

Cut the lamb into chunks. Marinate overnight in lemon juice, olive oil, garlic, ginger, diced onion and chilli. Drain the marinade and brown the meat on both sides in oil in a large pot. Add sultanas and almonds, chopped coriander and 1 cup of water or stock. Cover and simmer slowly for 1 hour 30 minutes, adding more water if necessary. Clean, halve and de-pip the apricots, and add to the pot. Carry on cooking for 15 minutes more. Serve with white, fluffy rice.

1 shoulder of lamb
juice of 1 lemon
1 tbs olive oil
2 cloves of garlic
3 cm stem ginger, grated
1 onion
1 red chilli, chopped
1 tbs sultanas
1 tbs almonds
a bunch of coriander
8 apricots

Children's Cactus Party

'My three (and let me add for those of you who don't read *Huisgenoot*) black grandchildren (my daughter Billie-Jeanne married Leroy, the son of the former president of my homeland, the Republic of Bapetikosweti) – Winnie-Jeanne, Nelson-Ignatius and La Toya-Ossewania Makoeloeli – just love giving this party for their friends. I encourage it because it gives them an opportunity to be artistic, the parties are great fun, the food is filling and everything can be cleaned up in no time at all.'

baguettes, rolls	Buy a variety of breads and rolls. Using a sharp knife, cut slits
round bread	in the bread and insert the Pringle chips at regular intervals.
almonds	Make small holes in the round bread, rolls and baguettes
pretzels	with a kebab stick and insert almonds and pretzels in lines to
Pringles	resemble cacti.
stick chips	Place bread in terracotta or zinc pots, half filled with sand
pots	and covered with kitchen paper.

Healthy party treats

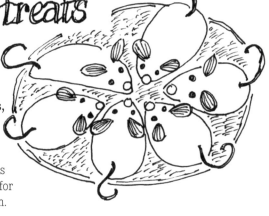

Pear mice meeting

A few pears, cut in half, liquorice strings, almonds, Smarties, grated coconut

Place pears in a circle on a bed of grated coconut. Use almonds for the ears, Smarties for the nose and liquorice string, cut to fit, for the tails and the eyes. Serve with ice cream.

Fresh & dried fruit kebabs

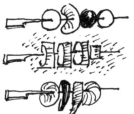

Skewer melon balls, orange segments, cherries and grapes.
   Do the same with pineapple chunks, then dust with grated coconut. This also works well with dried apricots, apples, peaches and pears.

Smoothies

Pulp various fruit – watermelon, strawberries, apricots, melon, peaches and bananas, pawpaw and mango. Yoghurt can be added.

Baked apple clowns

Core the apples and fill each hole with jam and sultanas. Place apples in an ovenproof dish and place a knob of butter on top of each one. Mix 6 tbs of sugar with 6 cups of water and pour into dish to cover apples halfway. Bake slowly at 180°C for 45 minutes or until apples are soft. Remove from oven to cool. Place a cone on top of each apple 'head' and decorate the faces. Use the cloves for eyes and secure a cherry with a toothpick for the nose.

6 apples, any kind
apricot jam
sultanas, raisins
butter
brown sugar
cones
whole cloves
cherries

Beachcombing

'Yzerfontein is only 20 minutes from Darling, so I often take my grandchildren there for the day. We picnic and strandloop and collect shells and driftwood for making things like picture frames and mobiles. I encourage them to collect their own lunch – it is great fun and also teaches them to be self-sufficient. Don't forget to buy a permit for collecting seafood and do take care not to exceed the official limits prescribed by the Marine Conservation officials.'

Mussel soup

Clean mussels, pull off the beards and put them into a large pot with chopped onions, garlic and parsley. Add half a bottle of dry white wine, cover and put on high heat to cook. The shells will start to open after 5 minutes. Discard those that don't open. Serve with crusty bread to soak up soup. Any leftover mussels can be used in a salad or pilaf, or preserved in the periwinkle marinade on this page to serve with drinks.

Sea urchins

Cut them in half with scissors (wear gloves). Spoon out the coral and discard the rest. The coral should be orange (not black) and smell of iodine. Eat raw with bread. The coral can also be used to flavour sauces, by pounding it into a paste and adding it to cream or butter – also good with scrambled eggs, or in an omelette. Add the coral of 4 sea urchins to 4 lightly beaten eggs. Heat butter in a pan and cook until set.

Periwinkles

Rinse well. Drop into boiling water and cook for about 6 minutes. Drain. Extract flesh by pulling it out with a pin or a fish hook. Cut off intestine and rinse. Eat fresh with garlic mayonnaise.

Put a few on slices of French loaf spread with garlic butter, and grill briefly in a hot oven until toast is crispy. Good with drinks.

You could also preserve them in a marinade – use 3 tbs olive oil and 1 tbs vinegar, 1 crushed clove of garlic, salt, pepper and a pinch of oregano.

14th July in Franschhoek

'It's no wonder that the French Huguenots chose to settle in this beautiful valley. The countryside must have reminded them of the hills and valleys of the country they were forced to leave. I always try to attend the celebrations, and simply cannot wait to taste French onion soup, coq-au-vin or daubé provençal. I know someone who collects snails from her vineyard, fattens them on lettuce leaves for a week and then makes the most delicious escargot in garlic butter, or a little ragout in red wine. Mimi's grandmother was a famous chef, and she passed down all her culinary secrets to her granddaughter, who even shared one with me: dried orange peel!'

French onion soup

Melt the butter and oil in a heavy-bottomed pot. Add onions and sauté over low heat, stirring from time to time. Add sugar and cook slowly until the onions are slightly caramelised. Add the beef stock, cover the pot and simmer for 30 minutes. Add a tot of brandy and season to taste. Serve in a soup tureen, or in individual soup bowls. Put toast on top of the soup and sprinkle with grated Gruyère cheese. Place tureen, or bowls, under the grill until the cheese melts and bubbles and turns a golden brown.

50 g butter
4 large onions, thinly
   sliced
1 tsp sugar
1 *l* beef stock
1 or 2 tots of brandy
French bread – sliced and
   toasted
Gruyère cheese

Rabbit in red wine

Heat oil in a large heavy-bottomed pot. Dust the rabbit pieces with flour. Sauté on all sides until brown. Remove from the pot. Sauté the bacon cubes and chopped onions until lightly browned, then return the rabbit to the pot and season. The French like to pour over a glass of cognac at this point and set it alight – make sure to keep away from the heat! When the flames subside, pour in the red wine and bring to the boil. Turn heat down and simmer. Add the thyme, orange peel, bay leaf and garlic and mix well. Cover and cook gently for 1 hour until the rabbit is tender and the sauce reduced. The sauce can be thickened with the mashed rabbit liver, a tsp of butter and a tsp of cornflour. Serve with tagliatelle pasta ribbons.

SERVES 6
1 rabbit, cut up (ask butcher
   for 6 or 8 pieces)
flour
100 g cubed bacon (lardons)
2 onions, coarsely chopped
1 bottle of good red wine
4 sprigs of thyme
dried orange peel
bay leaf
garlic

Apricot tart

Line a tart dish with the puff pastry and prick the bottom with a fork. Spread the compote over the pastry, then place the apricot halves on top. Mix the eggs, sugar and cream and pour over the apricots. Bake at 210°C for about 30 minutes. Sprinkle with toasted flaked almonds.

1 roll puff pastry
300 g apricot compote
600 g apricots, halved
3 eggs, 100 g sugar
200 ml cream
toasted flaked almonds

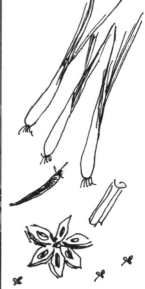

Indian Picnic

'I once went on a picnic with Jay Naidoo and his family. Gogo had made this great mince curry, which she transported in Tupperware, with stacks of naan bread. The most delicious carrot salad, yoghurt relish, chicken kebabs, meatballs called koftas, and egg curry are a few of the dishes I remember. Jay's Egyptian friend came too and brought a tin of dukkah which he had made himself. We spent the whole day discussing recipes with mama Naidoo, yours truly scribbling down the ingredients and eating in between. Here are some recipes I remember.'

Yoghurt relish

½ cup walnuts or cashews
2 cups natural yoghurt
2 tbs chopped fresh coriander
1 spring onion
1 small green chilli, finely chopped

Roughly crush the nuts. Combine all ingredients in a bowl and mix well. Season.

Variation: Instead of the coriander and walnuts, add finely diced cucumber and chopped fresh mint with a good pinch of ground cumin.

Mincemeat with peas

Heat oil in a large pan and sauté onion until golden brown. Add garlic, mincemeat, ginger, chilli, cumin, ground coriander and cayenne pepper. Add ½ cup of water and turn up the heat to boil, then cover, lower heat and simmer for 20 minutes. Add the peas, fresh coriander, salt, meat masala, lemon juice and another ½ cup of water. Stir and simmer on low heat for 10 minutes. Season to taste, adding salt and more lemon if necessary. Eat with vetkoek (p. 93) or puri (p. 43).

1 large onion, chopped
4 cloves of garlic, chopped
500 g minced beef
1 tbs grated ginger
1 green chilli, chopped
1 tsp ground cumin
1 tsp ground coriander
a pinch of cayenne pepper
1 cup frozen peas
a handful of fresh coriander
1 tbs lemon juice
1 tsp meat masala

Spicy vinegar eggs

Mash cloves of garlic. Combine ginger, cayenne pepper, cumin, salt, brown sugar and vinegar in a bowl. Mix well. Heat oil in a large pan. Add cinnamon stick and allow to sizzle for a few moments. Add the onion. Stir and sauté until onion is transparent. Add the spicy mixture, along with the masala. Stir to combine and cook for a few minutes. Add the water, stirring, and let the mixture simmer for 5 minutes to thicken. Put halved eggs in a flat dish and pour over the sauce to cover. Allow to cool. Pack into your picnic basket – and don't forget the bread.

4 cloves of garlic
2 tsp grated ginger
½ tsp cayenne pepper
1 tsp ground cumin
2 tbs brown sugar
2 tbs good wine vinegar
1 cinnamon stick
1 large onion, finely
  chopped
½ tsp masala
½ cup of water
6 hard-boiled eggs, halved

Dukkah

This is a dry mixture of crushed nuts, spices, salt and pepper. Eat with good bread dipped in olive oil as a snack, or you can sprinkle it over vegetables like grilled aubergine, or rice or chicken.

Roast the seeds in a dry pan for a few seconds. Roast the nuts in the dry pan – watch the pan so they don't burn. Pound the seeds and nuts until lightly crushed, but not powdered. Add salt and pepper. Sometimes dried herbs like marjoram or dry chilli powder can be added. Create your own special dukkah mix.

3 tbs sesame seeds
1 tbs cumin seeds
1 tbs coriander seeds
1 tbs peanuts
1 tbs almonds (or cashews
  or hazelnuts)
1 tsp salt and pepper

A Visit to Durban

'The wonderful thing about Indian cooking is using the enormous variety of spices and colours. Indian markets are a feast for the eyes! An Indian meal usually consists of a number of dishes – meat, vegetables, rice, pulses, chutney, salad, relish, yoghurt and fruit for dessert. I have eaten so many wonderful curries in my life and have asked for recipes from Delhi to Durbs. All the good chefs say the same thing: they use cumin, coriander, turmeric, black pepper, cardamom, cloves, cinnamon, fennel and mustard seed – and chillies to set everybody's tongues and palates alight. They all encouraged me to create and invent my own dishes and experiment, for instance, cook aubergine with cumin one day, then with fennel seed the next; use one spice or eight spices, depending on the dish. So here are a few spicy curries from my kitchen – and I wish you well to experiment too!'

Spicy Indian lamb

2 onions, chopped
1 green chilli, finely chopped
4 cloves of garlic, chopped
800 g cubed shoulder
    of lamb
1 tin tomatoes, chopped
1 tbs ground cumin

2 tsp ground coriander
1 tsp turmeric
½ tsp cayenne pepper
6 medium potatoes,
    peeled and halved
3 cups water

Heat sunflower oil in heavy-based pan. Put in onions, chilli and garlic. Stir and fry until onions are golden. Add meat and stir for about 5 minutes. Add tomatoes, cumin, coriander, turmeric, cayenne pepper and salt. Stir and cook for 10 minutes on high heat, until sauce thickens. Add potatoes and water. Cover and cook over low heat for about an hour, until meat is tender and sauce nice and thick. Serve with rice.

Potato & pea curry

Cut potatoes into large chunks. Heat mustard seeds in dry pan until they change colour and pop. Add oil and sliced onions and ginger and sauté, stirring, until transparent. Add the other spices until absorbed. Sprinkle with some of the mint, add potatoes and stir to coat. Add ½ cup of water, cover and simmer for 15 minutes. When the potatoes are soft, add peas and simmer for a further 5 minutes, until all the liquid has been absorbed. Sprinkle with the rest of the chopped fresh mint.

6 medium potatoes
2 tsp mustard seeds
2 onions, sliced
1 tbs grated ginger
1 tsp turmeric
chopped chilli
1 tsp curry powder
1 tsp fennel seeds
1 tsp ground cumin
garlic
chopped mint
1 cup frozen peas

Puri

Sift the flour and salt into a bowl. Separately mix oil and water. Blend into the flour to make a soft dough. Knead on a floured board until smooth and elastic. Form into a long roll. Break off small pieces. Roll out thinly into circles of about 10 cm in diameter. Deep-fry in hot oil until puffed up, crispy and golden. Drain on kitchen paper. Serve with curry. You can also cook these pastry circles in a dry nonstick pan for a minute to make Chinese pancakes.

1 cup cake flour
½ tsp salt
2 tbs sunflower oil
6 tbs water

Carrot salad

Put 2 tbs sunflower oil in a wok on medium heat. When oil is hot, put in the mustard seeds and as soon as they begin to pop and blacken, after a few seconds, add the grated carrots. Toss and stir-fry for a few minutes, adding the lemon juice, salt and pepper. The carrots should still be crunchy, but not raw. Serve hot or cold.

1 tbs mustard seeds
4 medium carrots, peeled and coarsely grated
2 tsp lemon juice

Bushveld Cuisine

'How can I explain those glorious safaris I went on with Pik? The early mornings in the bush, birdsong and cool breezes, sunsets through the thorn trees, the nights under the stars around the fire – and the Fierynecked Nightjar calling "Good Lord, deliver us ..." How intoxicating to watch Pik braai – such an expert. His eyes were always bigger than his tummy, so I came up with this dish.'

Bush cassoulet

bacon
onions
1 tin of butter beans
braai leftovers –
boerewors, steak,
chicken, etc.

Sauté bacon slowly in a pan to release fat. Remove and keep aside – then sauté onion rings gently in the fat until transparent. Add tinned butter beans, drained. Combine and stir. Add the bacon and braaied boerewors, cut into pieces, as well as cubes of steak or chicken left over from yesterday's braai. Turn off the heat. Cover the pan to keep warm to enhance the flavours.

Breakfast with bee-eaters

'After a morning drive, we sometimes stopped at a picnic spot for a late breakfast. We were usually starving, as we had been up from before dawn with only a quick coffee and beskuit. Pik knew how to make a fry-up in a skottel too! I've learnt so much from him ...'

bacon
boerewors
mushrooms
tomatoes
eggs

Fry bacon and boerewors until they sizzle. Add the mushrooms and tomatoes, cut in half. When all this is cooked, push to the side, then break the eggs and fry to your liking.

Of course, bee-eaters aren't always comrades that have been enriched by Black Economic Empowerment. (That's one of Pik's little jokes that I remember.) Sometimes bee-eaters are simply nothing but lovely little birds of the Bushveld. Ja-nee, Pik and I are still in touch. In fact, he faxes me every Friday.

Christmas in July at the Perron

Christmas Menu

'A little bit of what you fancy does you good, so eat, drink and be merry! Keep your Christmas simple – prepare as much as possible in advance to leave you time to enjoy yourself. Everyone loves a good roast – home cooking at its best – so prepare one or two stuffed roast chickens (p. 55), depending on the crowd you have to feed. We have found that over the years this has proved to be our clients' favourite food to this day, along with roast potatoes, butternuts and our own homemade bread.

The easiest way is to set up a buffet table and let your guests help themselves. This is what we do at The Perron – it contributes to a convivial, relaxed atmosphere. Here are some easy and affordable dishes to accompany roasts of your choice.'

Appetisers
Wrapped asparagus + Crudités p.19
Shrimp dip p.72
Salads
Courgette + Tomato p.21
Butternut + pasta p.22
Carrot p.43

Vegetables
Cauliflower cheese p.16
Pearl onions p.16
Herrenbone p.33
Potato gratin p.61
Spinach Rice p.77
Cinnamon Pumpkin p.77

Desserts
Apricot Tart p.39
Stuffed peaches p.67
Crunchy Chocolate Cake p.71
Strawberry delight p.73
Orange Trifle p.81
WITH COFFEE
Walnut Balls p.29

Kosher Dinner

'How I love to join my Jewish friends for their celebrations – marriages, bar mitzvahs, circumcisions, etc. Special dishes are prepared on religious holidays and, of course, the Ashkenazi traditional foods are different from those eaten in the Sephardic world. One must remember a few dietary laws when entertaining kosher friends. Dairy products are never eaten after meat. Pork, blood and crustaceans are forbidden. Wine, beer and alcohol are enjoyed with dinner. Maybe I should offer my kosher friends a South African meal, but I always enjoy the opportunity to make real Jewish food – and, when in doubt, to ask my friend Nowell Fine for advice.'

Potato latkes

500 g potatoes
1 egg

Peel and finely grate the potatoes. Put them in cold water. Drain. Wrap in a tea towel and wring out as much liquid as possible. Beat the egg. Add salt and grated potatoes and stir to mix well. In a nonstick frying pan, heat just enough oil to coat the bottom. Drop dessertspoonfuls of the mixture into the hot pan. Flatten and lower heat for potato cakes to cook through, turning to brown both sides. Serve immediately.

Pickled cucumbers

Pack cucumbers tightly in a jar. Bring water to boil with salt, garlic, peppercorns and dill and then pour over cucumbers to cover. Let it cool, cover and keep in the fridge for a week. Deliciously crunchy, it can be served as an apéritif or with chopped liver or herring.

1 kg small cucumbers
6 cups water
3 tbs coarse salt
4 cloves of garlic
10 black peppercorns
a bunch of dill

Chopped liver

Slowly sauté onion in fat until transparent and golden. Add the livers and cook for about 5 minutes or so. Remove from pan and cool. Using knife and fork, roughly chop up the livers with 1 boiled egg to make a coarse pâté. Season. Spread out onto a plate and garnish with the other egg which has been finely chopped. I add a little lemon juice to the mixture to enhance the flavour.

1 onion, chopped
chicken fat or sunflower oil
250 g chicken livers, deveined
2 hard-boiled eggs

Hungarian chicken

Buy chicken from a kosher butcher. Brown chicken pieces on both sides in chicken fat and remove from pan. Add onion in the same pan, sautéing slowly with the chopped red pepper until soft. Add tomatoes, sugar, paprika and chopped chilli and salt. Stir and mix together. Return chicken to pan, cover and simmer slowly for half an hour. You may add a little water if necessary. Serve with rice. I like to serve it with yellow rice (p. 78) for a sweet crunch and a bit of a South African flavour.

SERVES 6
6 chicken legs and thighs
3 tbs chicken fat
1 large onion, chopped
1 red pepper, in strips
1 tin tomatoes, diced
1 tsp sugar
2 tsp paprika
1 red chilli, chopped

Fruit Platter

grapes, pineapple, granadilla, watermelon, sweetmelon, pawpaw

Dinner with the President

'Oh, those heady days with Gorbachev – every dinner preceded by generous helpings of Beluga caviar and vodka. How can I forget the salty little eggs exploding against my palate – and thinking "I can feed every mouth in my homeland for the price of one apéritif?" Lumpfish roe is an affordable substitute and the President adores it. The last time he came to dinner I created this appetiser, whilst listening to Brenda Fassie singing "Black President".'

'Caviar' butter appetiser

100 g butter
2 tsp lumpfish roe

Mix softened butter and lumpfish roe with a fork. Roll into a roll. Wrap in clingwrap and put in the fridge to harden. When drinks have been poured, slice into rounds and serve with toast and a good vodka.

'Caviar' potatoes

Boil potatoes. Make a purée using a fork to mash, adding sour cream, chopped chives, salt and pepper. Turn out onto a plate and shape into an oval, with a flat top. Cover the top with as much 'caviar' as you like.

SERVES 2
4 medium potatoes
sour cream or crème fraîche
fresh chives
lumpfish roe

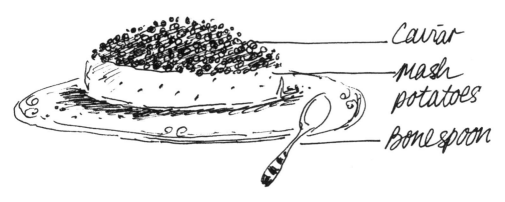

Caviar
mash
potatoes
Bone spoon

Beef stroganoff

Sauté sliced onions in 2 tbs of butter in a pan until transparent. Add mushrooms and cook for a few minutes. In a separate pan, melt 2 tbs of butter. Add the beef strips to the hot pan and stir-fry quickly to brown for no more than 5 minutes. Add a cup of white wine to the meat, then add the onions and mushrooms and the sour cream. Stir quickly over high heat to thicken. Add salt and pepper and sprinkle with paprika and parsley. Serve with pilaf rice.

400 g fillet or rump steak, cut into fine strips
2 onions, finely sliced
2 cups mushrooms, thinly sliced
1 cup sour cream
½ cup white wine
butter
paprika
parsley

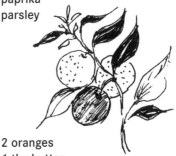

Caramelised oranges

Cut the oranges into wedges. Put the butter in a pan and heat. Add orange wedges and a cinnamon stick. Sprinkle with brown sugar and cook over high heat to caramelise. Once golden and syrupy, pour over a splash of Cointreau and cook quickly over high heat to evaporate the alcohol. Serve with Greek yoghurt and sprinkle with walnuts and dates.

These caramelised oranges can be used instead of fresh oranges in the orange trifle recipe (p. 81).

2 oranges
1 tbs butter
1 cinnamon stick
2 tsp brown sugar
Cointreau
walnuts
dates

National Treasures

Reconciliation bobotie

6 dried apricots
6 dried apple rings
½ cup seedless raisins
1 cup cold black tea
2 large onions,
   peeled and sliced

1 cup orange juice
1 tbs curry powder
2 tsp turmeric
1 kg minced beef
2 thick slices stale, white
   bread, crumbled

3½ tbs vinegar
4 eggs
½ cup milk
fresh lemon leaves

Soak the apricots, apple rings and raisins in the tea until soft. Drain the fruit, halve the apricots and cut the apple rings into pieces. Preheat the oven to 180°C. Grease an oven-proof dish well. Boil the onions in the orange juice until soft. Drain and fry lightly in olive oil. Add curry powder, turmeric, minced beef, breadcrumbs, vinegar, salt, pepper and soaked fruit. Mix lightly with a large fork and place in the dish. Beat the eggs and milk together and pour over the mixture. Fold a few lemon leaves into triangles and tuck them into the mixture. Bake the bobotie on the middle rack of the oven for 45 minutes, or until the egg 'custard' has set. Serve hot. Bobotie is always served with rice, chutney and sambals.

Koeksisters

500 g cake flour
2 tsp baking powder
4 tbs butter
2 eggs
1 cup milk

Syrup
1 kg sugar
2 cups water
½ tsp cream of tartar
2 cinnamon sticks
½ tsp ground ginger

First prepare the syrup. Heat sugar and water in a pan and stir until sugar has dissolved. Add the cream of tartar, cinnamon sticks and ginger and boil for a few minutes. Leave to simmer for 10 minutes, until it becomes syrupy. Transfer to a large bowl and allow to cool. Refrigerate for at least 6 hours.

   To prepare the dough, mix cake flour, baking powder and a pinch of salt in a large bowl. Rub in the butter, using your fingers, until it feels like breadcrumbs. Beat eggs and milk together and add to flour mixture. Knead into a dough. Form into a ball and cover with wax paper for 2 hours.

   Roll out dough to 1 cm thick. Cut into strips about 8 cm by 3 cm. Make two cuts, 1 cm from one end of the strip, so that you have 3 strips, attached at one end. Plait together and pinch to seal at the bottom.

   Heat cooking oil in a pan and deep-fry koeksisters for 2 minutes, until golden brown. Drain on kitchen paper for half a minute, then immerse in cold syrup until all air has escaped. Drain on a rack.

Visitor's Book

Desmond Tutu

Frene Ginwala

Helen Zille

Helen Suzman

Zulu Fans

Pik Botha

Charlize Theron

Tony Leon

'There is nothing more rewarding than surprising your oldest friends with something old, something new, something borrowed or maybe even something blue. (Blueberry juice over ice cream, perhaps?) Your table can always be your trump card. Or simply keep it predictably elegant. I used to get into trouble with BOSS in the old days: I kept telling them that I had a soft spot for red china. Of course they thought I meant those communists in Peking. Then I had to explain that it's just because it looks so gorgeous on a white tablecloth …'

Entertaining Ideas

Rösti

Peel and grate potatoes. Put in a tea towel and squeeze out the liquid. Cover oven tray with foil and coat with olive oil. Form 6 potato cakes with your hands and place on foil. Drizzle a little olive oil over the cakes, and sprinkle with salt and pepper. Bake at 180°C for 25 minutes, or until golden. If they brown too quickly, cover with foil during the course of baking. To serve, put a teaspoon of sour cream on the rösti, topped with the salmon eggs or roe.

SERVES 6
10 medium potatoes
sour cream
salmon eggs or lumpfish roe

Roast Chicken

When in doubt as to what to cook for a dinner party, you cannot go wrong roasting a whole farm chicken. For special occasions, a stuffing will contribute to a festive atmosphere – or serve it with a special sauce like green sauce. I cover the breast with lemon slices and cook it on a bed of rosemary sprigs as Sophia recommends. Add a handful of cloves of garlic and enough water to cover the bottom of the roasting dish. Roast for one and a half hours at 200°C. Serve with potatoes which have been tossed in duck fat, sprinkled with chopped rosemary and sea salt and roasted at the same time as the chicken in a separate ovenproof dish. Serve with vegetables in season.

Stuffing
2 cups breadcrumbs
1 egg
1 onion, chopped
1 tsp mixed herbs
Mix together well and stuff cavity of chicken.

Green sauce
2 tbs fresh parsley
2 spring onions, chopped
1 tsp capers
1 clove of garlic, crushed
2 tbs olive oil,
1 tbs vinegar, salt
1 tsp Dijon mustard
Combine and mix well.

Whole beef fillet

Marinate the fillet in garlic, soy sauce and olive oil for about 2 hours. Drain. Roast on a rack in a 220°C oven for half an hour. Remove and transfer to a serving platter. Slice into 25 mm thick pieces and place a knob of parsley butter in between the slices. Serve it with mustard and potato wedges. If you have any left over, use the next day. Place slices on a bed of mixed salad leaves with shavings of Parmesan cheese and the vinaigrette.

1.6 kg fillet
1 clove of garlic, crushed
4 tbs soy sauce
½ cup olive oil

Vinaigrette
1 tsp Dijon mustard
a pinch of salt, 2 tbs oil
½ tsp red wine vinegar
Mix everything together.

Guinea fowl

'Every now and then Oom Sampie brings me a guinea fowl – he has a flock on his farm. His wife uses the beautiful feathers to decorate lamp shades – we have such creative people living in our wonderful land. I can never decide how to cook guinea fowl, as I have two favourite recipes ... so I shall give you both.'

Guinea fowl in red wine

guinea fowl
2 onions, thyme
bay leaf, 5 juniper berries
red wine

Quarter the fowl, add sliced onions and braise very slowly in duck fat or oil. Add a bunch of thyme, a bay leaf, 5 juniper berries and a cup or two of good red wine and simmer for an hour and a half or so, depending on the age of the bird. Serve with red cabbage (p. 17) and roast potatoes.

...with sultanas & hanepoot

a handful of sultanas
1 cup hanepoot
6 carrots
2 onions

Soak the sultanas in the hanepoot or port for an hour. Chop up 6 carrots, add to the braising pot with the fowl and onions and simmer slowly for an hour. Add the sultanas and wine. Continue cooking slowly until fowl is tender. Serve with potato gratin (p. 61).

Roast quail

4 plump quail
thyme
2 cloves of garlic, chopped
1 leek
300 g mushrooms
putupap (p. 86)
a dash of cream

Season quail, sprinkling with thyme, salt and pepper. Place in an oiled roasting pan. To make sauce, sauté chopped leek in a little oil and butter for a few minutes. Add garlic, cream and sliced mushrooms and continue sautéing until mushrooms are cooked and liquid has evaporated. Season. Make putupap. About 10 minutes before putupap is ready, roast quail in a preheated oven at 220 °C for 20 minutes. Place a small mound of putupap on a plate and make an indent in the centre. Spoon in mushroom and leek sauce. Place whole roasted quail on top of its nest. You can also fry squares of flattened putupap in oil in a pan until crispy outside and soft and creamy inside, and serve the quail on top.

Oxtail stew

Lightly dust oxtail pieces with flour. Heat some oil in a large heavy-bottomed pot and brown the pieces on all sides. Add the red wine, bay leaves, allspice berries, cloves, thyme, orange peel, cloves of garlic (crushed), large carrots, salt and pepper. Bring to boil, then lower heat to simmer for 3 hours, adding a cup of beef stock (or water) to keep liquid.

Add pearl onions and baby carrots. Cook for a further 1 or 2 hours, or until meat is tender and falls off the bone. This stew is so much better prepared the day before, as the fat can easily be skimmed off before reheating, and it gives the flavours time to mingle and infuse the meat. Serve with rice or mashed potatoes.

1 kg oxtail
flour
1 cup red wine
thyme, 2 bay leaves
3 allspice berries
2 whole cloves
2 large carrots
orange peel
3 cloves of garlic
1 cup beef stock
20 pearl onions
15 baby carrots

Roast duck

'My old Chinese friend, Missi Hu, gave me a good tip on how to cook crispy duck – it remains my favourite way of preparing this delicious bird. Prick the skin all over and plunge the duck into boiling water for 2 minutes. Hang up to dry for a few hours. Make a paste using 2 tbs of soy sauce and 1 tbs of brown sugar and spread it onto the skin. Roast on a rack in a 220°C oven for one and a half hours.

Do not discard the fat that drips into the roasting pan below, but use it for roasting the potatoes – you will never eat them in any other way again – as the good news is that duck fat is very healthy.'

Orange sauce

Cut 2 oranges into thin slices. Soak 8 dried apricots. Roughly chop 1 onion. Put everything in a pot. Add 3 tbs of sugar and water to cover. Boil, then simmer for 30 minutes until soft and thick. Stir to break up apricots. Add 1 tbs red wine vinegar and a pinch of chilli.

Once cooked, the duck can be served in two ways – the traditional roast with ginger carrots, roast potatoes and orange sauce, or as Peking duck, which is served with pancakes, cucumbers, spring onions and plum sauce.

Peking duck

cucumbers, cut into strips
spring onions, shredded
Hoisin or plum sauce

Cut the meat and the crispy skin into thin strips and place on a platter. Pile pancakes on a side dish. Place cucumber strips and shredded spring onions in separate bowls, alongside the Hoisin or plum sauce. To eat, take pancake and cover with the sauce. Place the skin and meat strips onto this. Add cucumber and spring onion and roll up pancake. This is a most sublime taste experience.

Chinese pancakes

Place flour in a large bowl and gradually stir in the hot water and oil. Mix into a dough, adding more water if mixture seems dry. Knead dough until smooth, dusting with flour if it becomes sticky. Form into a roll, cut off small pieces. Using a rolling pin, roll out dough to make pancake circles 12 cm in diameter and 2 mm thick.

1 cup flour
1 cup hot water
2 tbs peanut oil

Pan-fry both sides in a hot pan without oil for a minute. Pancakes must be supple, but cooked through.

Roast leg of lamb

Using a sharp knife, cut small slits in the meat. Press the garlic slices into the slits and do the same with the rosemary. Place the lamb into a roasting tray on a bed of rosemary sprigs and a handful of cloves of garlic. Add a cup of water to the tray. Roast in preheated oven at 200°C for 1 hour if you like it pink, or ½ an hour longer for more well-done. Lamb goes well with grilled aubergine, heerenbone or roast potatoes – you choose!

1.8 kg leg of lamb
4 cloves of garlic, sliced
sprigs of rosemary

Rack of pork with pears

Squeeze lemon juice over pork. Place in a roasting dish with ½ cup of water. Grill for 10 minutes – take care not to burn. In the meantime, peel the pears and cut into quarters. Wash potatoes and cut in half. Peel onions and cut into 8 sections each. Take out the pork dish and spoon the cooking juices over the roast. Place the pears, potatoes and onions into the roasting dish with the pork. Sprinkle with mixed herbs, salt and pepper, drizzle over olive oil and return to the oven. Roast at 180°C for 40 minutes.

juice of ½ lemon
800 g pork rack
2 pears
12 small new potatoes
2 medium onions
1 tsp mixed herbs

Whole Cape salmon

Score the cleaned gutted fish three or four times on both sides. Place fish in a baking dish which has been lined with foil. Stuff cavity with fresh herbs, garlic, salt and pepper. Squeeze lemon juice and drizzle olive oil all over the fish. Bake in a 200°C oven for 30 minutes. Turn up grill to blister the skin for about 10 minutes. Stir-fry vegetables in 1 tbs oil in a hot wok, adding soy sauce and lemon juice. Scatter vegetables over fish to serve.

whole Cape salmon
fresh thyme and oregano
1 clove of garlic, chopped
soy sauce
lemon juice, olive oil
carrots and courgettes, cut
  into thin strips
broccoli florets
spring onions, chopped
mangetout

Graça's Lunch

'When I was young, I used to go on holiday to Lourenço Marques with my friends. Hasie borrowed his uncle's Buick and we all piled in. We couldn't afford the Polana Hotel, but stayed in a shack on the beach. All those happy memories came flooding back when I tasted that wonderful food at Graça's again.'

Hot garlic prawns

24 prawns
5 whole peri-peri
2 tsp salt
1 tbs parsley
6 cloves of garlic, crushed
2 tbs olive oil

Make a marinade with all the ingredients and coat prawns with it. Leave to marinate for 2 hours. Heat 1 tbs oil in a large frying pan and shallow-fry prawns for 3 minutes. Serve with garlic sauce – melt ½ cup butter in a small pan. Add 2 chopped cloves of garlic and 2 whole peri-peri and heat for 2 minutes. Do not burn the garlic! Add 1 tbs lemon juice and mix well. Also delicious on the braai. Grill over moderate coals for 5 minutes.

Rosemary Basting Brush

Chicken peri-peri

4 baby chickens
5 whole peri-peri, crushed
2 tsp lemon juice
4 cloves of garlic, crushed
1 tsp paprika
2 tbs soft butter
2 tbs olive oil
salt and pepper

Spatchcock the chickens by cutting open through the back and flattening down with your hand. Make a paste with all the other ingredients and spread it over chicken, inside and out. Leave to marinate for 2 hours. Grill in oven, basting with marinade when turning – or cook on the braai for that lovely smoky flavour. Serve with hot garlic peri-peri sauce as above.

Bom Dia !

Great Gratins

Onion gratin

Slice onions finely. Sauté in a mix of 1 tbs of butter and 1 tbs oil, stirring regularly for about 25 minutes, until transparent and all liquid has evaporated. Grate Parmesan cheese. Heat oven to 180°C. Butter a gratin dish and spoon in onions. Sprinkle Parmesan over the onions. Bake for 20 minutes until top is browned. Serve immediately with roast lamb, chicken or beef – or with baguette, as a starter.

8 large onions
2 tbs butter
4 tbs grated Parmesan cheese

Courgette gratin

Grate courgettes and place in a bowl. Add the grated Gruyère, salt, pepper, beaten egg and cream. Mix together thoroughly. Transfer to a greased ovenproof dish and bake at 180°C for 35 minutes.

4 large courgettes
150 g Gruyère cheese
1 egg, 1 cup cream

Fennel gratin

Remove feathery top growth and outer leaves from fennel and keep for soup or stockpot. Cut bulbs into quarters. Place in a pan or pot with a little water, cover and poach until al dente – about 10 minutes – adding water to keep moist. Drain and transfer to an ovenproof dish. Spoon over crème fraîche and sprinkle over Parmesan. Place under hot grill for 8 minutes or so until golden brown and bubbling.

4 fennel bulbs
1 cup crème fraîche
4 tbs grated Parmesan

Potato gratin

Peel potatoes and cut into 3 mm thick slices. Butter bottom of a gratin dish and layer potato slices. Season well with salt, pepper and rosemary in between the layers. Pour over milk and cream. Cover with foil, pierced with a few holes. Bake for an hour at 190°C, or until potatoes are soft. Remove foil and brown under grill.

You can use chicken stock instead of the milk and cream for a kosher meal. This also goes well with grilled meat.

1 kg potatoes
20 g butter
chopped rosemary
1 cup milk
½ cup cream

Evita Dines with Evita

'"After the captains and the kings have departed" I soothe my spirits with a cocktail and think how I shall cook myself a meal with delicacy so that I can dine in solitude and reflect upon the world's problems. I take special care preparing a meal when Evita is dining with herself. Time to experiment maybe, or cook an old favourite – then peace and quiet to savour each mouthful without having to talk or entertain. These are my special moments to replenish myself for battle on another day ...'

Marrow bones on toast

Gently poach two marrow bones in a little water for about 5 minutes – do not boil. Remove from pan and drain. Take out marrow with a spoon and spread on hot, crisp, dry toast. Sprinkle with sea salt, black pepper and chopped parsley and eat immediately – a feast for one!

Salmon fillet

Pan-fry a good piece of salmon in a little butter and oil over medium heat, skin-side down, for about 5 minutes. Cover and let it steam for a further 5 to 10 minutes. Serve on horseradish mashed potato (recipe below).

Salmon tartare

1 piece of fresh salmon
olive oil
lemon
2 tbs cream cheese
1 tsp capers
fresh coriander, chives

Cut fresh salmon into chunks. Drizzle olive oil over and a squeeze of lemon. Mix with cream cheese and capers. Add fresh chopped coriander and chives, salt and pepper. Cover and chill for 2 hours. Serve on a green salad with toast.

Horseradish mashed potato

4 potatoes
2 tbs cream, 1 tbs butter
2 tsp horseradish
chopped chives

Peel and cook potatoes in salted boiling water. When soft, drain and mash in a dish incorporating the cream, butter, chives and horseradish. Mix well and season. Cover and keep warm until ready to serve.

Sophia Comes to Stay

'Involtini, capellini, tortellini, risotto, fagioli, peperonata, frittata, crostini, bruschetta, fettunta, melanzane, pasta, pasta, pasta and conviviality. That's what Sophia brought with her when she came to stay – all I know about Italian cooking, I owe to her ...'

How to cook pasta

Cook spaghetti, etc. in well-salted, boiling water. As soon as you drop the pasta into the water, stir well to separate the pasta and carry on stirring throughout the cooking time. Taste and remove from heat as soon as it is almost al dente. Toss with its sauce over low heat as it continues to soften. Keep a cup of the pasta water aside to dilute the sauce if necessary.

Tomato sauce

1 kg plum (or tinned) tomatoes
2 cloves of garlic, chopped
1 tbs chopped onion
1 tbs chopped parsley
1 tbs chopped carrot
1 tbs chopped celery
⅓ cup oil, 1 tbs sugar

A 'soffrito' consists of a little onion, celery, carrot and various herbs and is the basis of many a good sauce to go with pasta, vegetables, fish or meat.

Pour boiling water over tomatoes in a bowl and leave for a minute. Peel and quarter. Make the soffrito. Slowly sauté garlic, onion, parsley, carrot and celery in a little oil until onions are transparent. Add chopped tomatoes, sugar and seasoning. Cover to cook over low heat, stirring now and then, until all water has evaporated – about 1 hour, maybe more.

Use as sauce for anything you like. Most delicious in the following antipasto.

Tomato
mozzarella
Basil

Antipasto

Spoon tomato sauce over grilled aubergine rounds, grate Parmesan over and garnish with black olives. Cover grilled aubergine rounds with mozzarella and tomato slices and top with basil leaves.

Vegetable frittata

'This is an Italian-style omelette, which is usually thick and flat and filled with pasta or vegetables in season. It can be served hot or cold and is perfect for picnics, as a light lunch with a salad, as a first course, or cut into small squares to serve as an appetiser.'

Beat the eggs in a large bowl with salt and pepper. Add cooked vegetables, cheese and herbs and mix well. Heat oil in a medium-sized pan. When hot, pour in the mixture. Cook until frittata is golden and set at the bottom. You can now either tip the frittata onto a plate and slide it back onto the pan to cook the other side, or you can place the pan under a hot grill until the top is set and golden brown, which is easier, and the way I cook it.

4 large eggs
2 cups cooked broccoli florets
1 cup cooked green beans, chopped
2 tbs grated Parmesan cheese
1 tsp oregano
1 tbs chopped parsley

Figs & mozzarella

4 fresh, ripe but firm figs
4 mozzarella balls
balsamic vinegar
sweet wine

Cut the figs into slices. Cut mozzarella balls into rounds. Arrange on a serving platter, alternating layers.

For a first course, sprinkle good balsamic vinegar, sea salt and black pepper. For dessert, pour over a dash of sweet white wine and grill for 2 minutes.

Peperonata

2 medium onions
2 large red peppers
2 large yellow peppers
2 cloves of garlic, chopped
2 large tomatoes
1 tsp oregano
basil leaves

Heat 3 tbs olive oil in a pan and sauté roughly chopped onions for 5 minutes. Deseed the peppers and cut into squares. Add peppers, garlic and salt to the onions and stir to mix. Continue cooking over low heat. Add roughly chopped tomatoes and oregano. Cover and cook slowly, stirring from time to time, until peppers are just cooked. Sprinkle with fresh basil leaves. Serve hot or cold, with fish, meat or as a pasta sauce.

Variation: Add chunks of courgette and a beaten egg and stir to combine. Delicious on its own, or with bread.

Chicken livers & onions

2 red onions
250 g chicken livers, trimmed
balsamic vinegar

Heat 2 tbs olive oil in a large frying pan. Add chopped onions and sauté for 5 minutes. Then add the chicken livers over high heat until browned. Add a splash of balsamic vinegar. Don't overcook the livers, as this dries them out. Try to keep them pink in the middle. Season. Serve tossed with pasta or rice, or spoon over a bed of salad leaves. Delicious as a topping for bruschetta, or putupap – polenta style.

Potato pizza

Boil potatoes. Peel and mash. Add the sifted flour, a pinch of salt and eggs. Mix. Spoon onto a large greased ovenproof plate and flatten. Bake in a 200°C oven for 20 minutes. In the meantime, slice the onions and sauté in oil until golden. Mix with egg in a bowl. Remove potato base from oven. Cover with the onion mixture. Decorate with tomato slices, black olives and Parmesan cheese and a sprinkling of oregano. Put back in the oven and cook for 20 minutes or until topping is bubbling and sides cooked. You can try other toppings – feta cheese, bacon, anchovies, whole garlic – whatever you fancy.

2 medium, floury potatoes
2 tbs flour, 2 eggs

Topping
2 medium onions
1 egg, 1 tomato
8 black olives
2 tbs grated Parmesan
  cheese
a sprinkling of oregano

Spring pasta

Heat 2 tbs olive oil in a large pan. Add chopped leek and garlic and sauté for 3 minutes. Add peas, asparagus tips, courgettes cut into sticks and baby spinach to the pan. Stir well and cook for 3 minutes. Put the tagliatelle in salted, boiling water and stir while cooking. In the meantime, stir the cream into the vegetables over low heat and simmer for 3 minutes. Drain pasta. Add to vegetable pan. Season and sprinkle with Parmesan cheese and basil leaves and toss well. Serve at once.

1 leek, 1 clove of garlic
½ cup fresh peas
12 asparagus tips
8 small courgettes
2 handfuls baby spinach
400 g tagliatelle
½ cup cream
5 tbs freshly grated
  Parmesan cheese
basil leaves

Stuffed peaches

Blanch and then skin peaches. Cut in half and remove pip. Mash one peach with a fork and mix with crushed macaroons and brandy. Fill peach halves with this mixture. Place in an ovenproof dish. Pour wine over and sprinkle with sugar. Bake in a moderate oven until tender – about 10 minutes.

5 lovely peaches
4 tbs crushed macaroons
1 tbs brandy
1 cup white wine
3 tbs sugar

Greek Visits

'When I used to visit Melina Mercouri – always on a Sunday – she would prepare the most delicious and simple Greek food. Sometimes she would sing as she cooked (my favourite was "Love Theme" from *Phaedra*). Once or twice Theodorakis popped in. Melina's skordalia was a heavenly garlicky cloud, which we used to eat with bread, while sipping retsina.

For entertaining Greek style, I like to make lots of mezze. Many people like to taste bits and pieces of a wide variety of interesting food, rather than a *bord kos*. Buy pitta and good crusty breads, give your guests a glass of ouzo, play Greek music and try some of these *mezethes* – and hope the guests don't break the plates!'

Classic Greek salad

Tomatoes, cucumber, onions, feta cheese, black olives, oregano, olive oil

Quarter 2 ripe tomatoes. Cut cucumber into chunks and a sweet onion into rings. Mix together and place in a serving dish. Cut feta cheese into slabs and place on top. Add black olives. Sprinkle oregano and drizzle a lot of good olive oil over the salad. Eat with bread as a first course.

Skordalia

500 g potatoes, 3 cloves of garlic, olive oil, lemon juice

Boil potatoes. Peel and mash. Warm crushed garlic in olive oil to soften. Mix into mash, adding lemon juice and salt. Mix and stir until soft and creamy, and season to taste. Spoon onto a plate, drizzle olive oil over and sprinkle with paprika. Delicious as a dip with fried or grilled fish and vegetables.

Tzatziki

1 cucumber, peeled, seeded and grated, 300 ml Greek yoghurt, 3 cloves of garlic, crushed, olive oil, chopped mint

Salt the cucumber and leave in colander to drain for an hour. Squeeze out all the liquid and put in a bowl. Add the yoghurt and mix with garlic and cucumber. Combine well with a tablespoon of good olive oil. Taste and season. Sprinkle with chopped mint.

This is excellent with crusty bread, but can also be served with cold lamb, or with meatballs, aubergine or any rice dish.

Grilled aubergine

Cut aubergine lengthwise. I never bother salting the slices, but just drizzle with oil and place under a hot grill for 10 minutes, both sides, until nicely browned. Arrange on a platter and serve with garlic yoghurt or tomato sauce.

Aubergine caviar

3 large aubergines, 2 cloves of garlic,
lemon juice, olive oil

Ideally aubergine should be roasted over a
braai to charcoal the skin, giving the flesh
a lovely smoky aroma. Otherwise, prick the
skin and roast in an oven at 180°C for an
hour. Spoon out the flesh into a bowl. Add the
garlic, juice of half a lemon, salt and pepper
and olive oil. Blend together to make a purée.

Tomato sauce

1 tsp cumin seeds
1 tsp fennel seeds
400 g tinned tomatoes, chopped
1 tbs tomato purée, ½ cup water
a pinch of oregano, 1 tsp sugar

Heat olive oil in a large pan. Add cumin and
fennel seeds and allow to sizzle for a minute,
until quite aromatic. Add tomatoes and water
and stir. Add tomato purée, oregano, sugar,
salt and pepper and simmer for 10 minutes.

Meatballs

2 slices of white bread
500 g minced beef or lamb
1 tbs ground cumin, 1 egg, lightly beaten
2 cloves of garlic, crushed
flour for dusting

Soak bread in water. Drain and squeeze
dry. Put mince in a large bowl with cumin,
egg and garlic. Add the bread. Season and
mix well. Roll small handfuls into short,
thin sausage shapes. Dust lightly with flour.
Heat oil in a nonstick pan and fry meatballs
in batches until golden all round. Drain on
kitchen paper. These meatballs can also be
cooked by simmering in tomato sauce.

Fried courgettes

4 medium courgettes, 2 tbs flour

Cut courgettes lengthwise into thin strips.
Dust with flour. Heat sunflower oil in a nonstick pan and fry courgette slices for a minute
or two until golden. Turn over to brown other
side. Remove and drain on kitchen paper.
Season. Serve with a bowl of tzatziki.

Vegetarian Lunch

'Most vegetarians eat grains and food made from grains – rice, corn and pasta dishes are daily fare – along with pulses like beans, chickpeas, lentils, etc. Add to these vegetables and fruit in season, cheese and eggs, as well as a healthy imagination, and you have endless possibilities for combinations of flavours and colours. For your strictly vegetarian friends, don't use chicken stock or gelatine in any of the dishes you serve them. As I am passionate about vegetables and also eat a vegetarian meal quite often, it always gives me pleasure to create new combinations and not just serve the usual lentil loaf.'

Appetisers

Stuff cherry tomatoes with egg mayonnaise. Sprinkle with chopped chives. Serve with aubergine caviar (p. 69) and cucumber wedges sprinkled with cumin.

Courgette dip

Cut 4 small baby courgettes into rounds and steam these in a little water until soft. Drain. Mash with a fork and add 1 tbs cream cheese, crushed garlic and chilli. Season and mix well.

Lettuce rolls

Shred the vegetables and place in a bowl with a marinade of soy sauce, oil, ginger, garlic and lemon juice for 1 hour or so. Drain. Separate the leaves of an iceberg lettuce, wash and dry. Bind the vegetables with mayonnaise flavoured with chilli and chopped coriander. Fill the lettuce leaves with this mixture and roll up like a spring roll. Arrange on a platter and serve with sweet chilli dipping sauce. It could be fun to let each guest fill the rolls themselves.

1 carrot, 1 courgette
1 red pepper, 4 spring onions
50 g bean sprouts
2 tbs soy sauce, 2 tbs olive oil
1 tbs grated ginger
1 clove of garlic, chopped
½ lemon, 1 iceberg lettuce
mayonnaise, 1 chilli, chopped
fresh coriander

Sweet chilli dipping sauce

1 tbs soy sauce
1 spring onion, finely chopped
2 tbs wine vinegar
2 tsp sesame oil
1 tbs castor sugar

2 tsp grated ginger
1 small chilli, finely chopped

Mix together in a bowl with 1 tbs of water.

Thai green curry

Pour coconut milk into a pot. Add the curry paste and heat gently. Stir over low heat to mix. Cut vegetables into bite-sized pieces, season and add to the coconut milk. Cook for a few minutes, then test if all vegetables are al dente. Serve the curry, sprinkled with fresh coriander, with basmati rice or noodles. For your non-vegetarian friends, add chicken breast strips halfway through cooking the vegetables.

1 tin coconut milk
1 packet green curry paste
200 g green beans
200 g broccoli florets
4 medium courgettes
100 g cabbage strips
1 sweet potato
fresh coriander

Crunchy chocolate cake

Crush the biscuits and soak them in the Grand Marnier. Melt the chocolate in a pot over hot water. Remove from heat and slowly beat in egg yolks and soft butter. Cool. Whip cream until stiff and gently fold it into the mixture. Butter a springform tin, line the bottom with buttered baking paper and spoon in some of the chocolate mixture. Smooth down, and then add a layer of the biscuit mixture. Repeat twice. Refrigerate for 6 hours to set. Sprinkle a little icing sugar on top, and decorate with glacé orange peel.

250 g macaroon biscuits
3 tbs Grand Marnier
500 g dark chocolate
2 egg yolks
120 g butter
1 heaped cup double cream

Diabetics Come to Dinner

'Nowadays everyone seems to know someone who is diabetic, so when inviting these friends, remember to find out the type of diabetes they suffer from and limit the amount of sugar used. Always serve food with the apéritif – a tasty appetiser which will line the stomach. Food slows down the absorption of alcohol into the bloodstream. This allows the liver to process glucose much better while handling the alcohol. Diabetics should only have one drink a day, so should be encouraged to nurse it all evening. A vodka with pure, fresh grapefruit juice should do the trick.'

Butternut pâté

Roast butternut. Cool, mash roughly. Mix 1 cup of cream cheese, crushed garlic and chopped chilli, and add to butternut. Season and mix well with 2 tbs roughly chopped pistachio nuts. Serve on hot toast.

Shrimp dip

Mix together 2 tbs low-fat cream cheese, 2 tbs fat-free yoghurt, 2 tbs shrimps (fresh or tinned), 2 drops of Tabasco and 1 tbs chopped chives, salt and pepper. Serve with toast or crackers, cucumber sticks or chicory leaves.

Cucumber soup

Grate the cucumber, put into a colander and sprinkle with salt. Allow to drain for an hour or so. Wash off the salt and drain once more. Beat the yoghurt, crème fraîche, garlic, dill, olive oil and cucumber together in a large serving bowl. Season to taste with salt and white pepper. Chill before serving – a most refreshing soup.

2 cucumbers, peeled and grated
4 cups plain yoghurt
½ cup crème fraîche
2 cloves of garlic, crushed
½ tsp dill, 1 tbs olive oil
white pepper

Moroccan chicken

In a large heavy-bottomed pan, heat oil and add spices – cumin, paprika, turmeric and cinnamon and cook for a minute. Add the chicken thighs in batches, browning both sides. Transfer to a large casserole. Add chopped onion and garlic to the pan and sauté slowly until golden. Add to the chicken in the casserole. Add a cup of water and the apricots to the pan. Bring to the boil and cook for 5 minutes. Pour this over the chicken in casserole, with ½ cup of fresh coriander. Bring to boil, cover and simmer for 30 minutes, until chicken is cooked. Sprinkle in almonds and more coriander. Serve with couscous.

To serve, spoon couscous onto a large platter and place chicken pieces on top with sauce. Garnish with coriander. Serve with glasses of iced mint tea.

1 tsp ground cumin
1 tsp paprika
1 tsp turmeric
1 cinnamon stick
6 chicken thighs
1 large onion
4 cloves of garlic
1 cup dried apricots
fresh coriander
½ cup slivered almonds

Couscous

Bring 1 cup of salted water to the boil, adding 1 tsp of oil. Remove from heat and add 1 cup of couscous. Cover and let it swell for 5 minutes. Add 1 tsp of butter and return to low heat for 1 minute, stirring with a fork to break up lumps.

Strawberry delight

Mix mascarpone and orange juice in a bowl. Blend half the strawberries to make a coulis. Cut the rest of the strawberries into small chunks. Make the dessert in 4 glasses. Layer bottom with a spoonful of mascarpone. Add chopped strawberries, followed by another layer of mascarpone. Spoon over coulis and top with crème fraîche, a whole strawberry and sprig of mint.

1 cup mascarpone
4 tbs fresh orange juice
500 g strawberries
½ cup crème fraîche
mint sprigs

Padkos

'Padkos is a very important part of travelling, as I am not keen on stopping at petrol station cafés when I'm hungry – so much more relaxing to find a picnic table under a tree where I can spread out my tablecloth and my own homemade delights. So the night before I set off on a journey, I cook up a storm as one never knows what is in store ...'

Bambi bobotie

1 large onion
2 tsp curry powder
1 tsp turmeric
300 g mincemeat
1 tbs fine semolina
2 tsp lemon juice
1 bay leaf
2 eggs, a little milk
2 tbs chopped, dried apricots
2 tbs sultanas
2 tbs chopped peanuts

Custard topping
1 egg, 1 tbs milk
½ tsp turmeric

I cannot travel without bobotie, so I've simplified my recipe. I also make it this way for cocktail parties – cut into squares.

Sauté onion until soft. Add curry powder and turmeric and fry for 2 minutes. Add mincemeat and cook over medium heat, adding the semolina and lemon juice, salt and pepper. Cover and cook for 15 minutes. In a bowl, mix the eggs, milk, chopped apricots, sultanas and peanuts. Add the meat mixture and mix lightly with a fork. Turn into a small greased ovenproof dish and press a bay leaf on top. For the topping, beat egg with a little milk and turmeric. Pour over bobotie and bake at 180°C for 45 minutes until it is set and golden and pulls away from the sides of the dish.

Pasta frittata

2 eggs, 2 cups cooked spaghetti
2 tbs tomato sauce
2 tbs grated Parmesan cheese
1 tbs chopped parsley

Beat the eggs in a large mixing bowl. Add the spaghetti, tomato sauce, cheese, parsley, salt and pepper and mix well. Heat oil in a smallish nonstick frying pan. When hot, pour in the egg mixture. Cook until frittata is golden brown and set at the bottom. Remove pan from heat and place under a hot grill until top is set and golden. This is delicious eaten cold or at room temperature, so it is perfect for padkos and picnics.

Butterbean purée

1 400 g tin of butter beans
1 tbs chopped parsley
lemon juice to taste, 4 tbs olive oil
2 tbs crunchy peanut butter
1 tbs chopped peanuts

Drain the butter beans. Mash with a fork and mix in parsley, lemon juice and olive oil to make a rough pâté mixture. Mix in the peanut butter and peanuts. Season. Spoon into a jar to transport. Use as a spread on bread or with cucumber slices – also a very healthy snack for the kids.

Sunday Lunch

'That wicked Oscar Wilde seems to say everything first: "After a good dinner, one can forgive anybody, even one's own relatives." Ja-nee.

I try to get my family together at least one Sunday in the month, which is difficult, because they are scattered far and wide across the land. De Kock and his friend Moff de Bruyn live in Pretoria (which they call Tshwane), Izan is still on the farm helping Eugene stay on his horse for more than a minute, while Billie-Jeanne and Leroy travel wherever the presidential jet takes them. The grandchildren spend more time with me, and that is the ultimate challenge: to cook so well and with so much imagination that they don't take smses during the meal, or want to Google anything. It is also my duty as their Gogo to insist that eating happens at the dining table, not in front of the television from a Nando's bag!'

Mieliekoekies

1 cup self-raising flour 1 onion, chopped 2 tsp turmeric 2 tsp ground cumin 1 tsp salt 1 cup shredded spinach or lettuce leaves 1 cup sweetcorn kernels	Sift flour into a mixing bowl. Add onion, turmeric, cumin powder, salt and spinach and combine with enough water to make a thin, lumpy batter. Add a cup of sweetcorn and mix well. The batter must not be too thick, but run off a spoon slowly. Heat oil in deep nonstick frying pan and drop in tablespoons of batter. Wait until batter forms little holes, then turn to brown the other side for a minute or two. Drain on kitchen paper. Eat hot. Double the quantity if the kids want more!

Darling chicken pie

Roast a plump farm chicken for 1½ hours at 200°C.
When cool, remove skin and bones and cut flesh into small
chunks. Make chicken stock with the bones (p. 11), adding
the fennel seeds, cinnamon stick, orange peel, cloves and
garlic. In a pan, sauté chopped onion in butter and oil until
soft. Add Maizena and stir to incorporate. Add 2 ladles of
chicken stock, stirring well to combine. Add the lemon zest,
lemon juice and white wine and simmer, stirring until sauce
thickens and bubbles. Beat egg and mix in with the chicken
pieces in a bowl. Grate over nutmeg, add this to the sauce
and mix well. Season. Spoon half the mixture into a large
ovenproof pie dish and top with quartered hard-boiled eggs.
Cover with remaining filling mixture – allow to cool. Cover
with pastry and seal the edges. Prick the pastry with a fork.
Brush with beaten egg. Bake at 200°C for 30 minutes or until
golden. Serve with spinach rice (recipe below) or yellow rice
(p. 78) and a sambal of tomato and onion.

1.6 kg farm chicken
1 tsp fennel seeds
1 cinnamon stick
orange peel
3 whole cloves
3 cloves of garlic
1 large onion
1 tbs butter
1 tbs Maizena (cornflour)
chicken stock
1 tsp lemon zest
1 tsp lemon juice
2 tbs white wine
1 egg, nutmeg
2 hard-boiled eggs
230 g roll flaky pastry

Spinach rice

Heat a little oil in a heavy-based pot. Add rice and stir to coat.
Add stock and salt and bring to the boil. Reduce heat and
simmer, covered, for 20 minutes, until cooked. Set aside. Heat
oil in a separate pot and add the chopped onions. Stir and
sauté until transparent. Add the spinach, cover pot and leave
to cook for about 5 minutes. Add the chopped spring onions
and garlic.

   Mix well. Add this mixture to the rice and stir. Can be
served hot or at room temperature with grilled chicken, or
fried fish. Also delicious as a humble dish on its own with
crumbled feta cheese and dill, and extra olive oil dribbled
over – or with garlic yoghurt.

1 cup long-grain rice
2 cups stock
2 large onions, chopped
250 g spinach, chopped
   (fresh or frozen, thawed)
4 spring onions
2 cloves of garlic, chopped

Cinnamon pumpkin

Peel and deseed the pumpkin and chop into chunks. Place in
a pot with a cup of water. Add the sugar and cinnamon and
boil until the pumpkin is soft and the water has evaporated.
Sprinkle with a pinch of salt, add butter and mash.

600 g pumpkin
1 tsp sugar
2 tsp ground cinnamon
1 tsp butter

'I like to use borrie as I love the rich yellow colour – let the sun shine in, is what I say. And when the kids bring their friends and there are so many more mouths to feed, I reach for the pasta – baby pasta shells, or mini bowtie pasta – and just combine it with whatever vegetables I'm serving, like peas or butternut. I sprinkle chopped peanuts over this – and they love it!'

Yellow rice

1 small onion
3 cups basmati rice
6 cups water
1 tsp turmeric
1 cinnamon stick
3 cardamom pods
1 tbs currants or raisins
1 chicken stock cube

Sauté chopped onion in a little oil in a heavy-bottomed pot for a minute. Add rice and stir to coat. Add water, turmeric, cinnamon, cardamom, currants and chicken stock cube. Bring to boil. Simmer until water has evaporated and small holes appear in the rice. The rice should be cooked in 15 minutes. Remove from heat. Cover with a clean tea towel and place lid on top. Let it rest for 5 to 10 minutes before serving. This dries out the rice, preventing it from becoming soggy or sticky.

'And when the kids' friends bring their parents, it is essential to have a few tricks up your sleeve. I always make too much rice anyway, so I find stir-fries are the answer in emergencies like these. I make it look as if I planned the lunch this way! Make sure you always have chicken breasts in the freezer (otherwise someone has to run to the Spar).'

Ginger chicken stir-fry

Cut chicken breasts into thin strips. Squeeze over lemon juice, and grate the ginger. Heat oil in a wok and add ginger. Stir for a few seconds. Add chicken and stir-fry for 5 minutes. Add a dash or two of soy sauce, chopped spring onions and a little water to moisten. Scatter a handful of roughly chopped peanuts at the end, and fresh coriander.

4 chicken breasts
1 lemon
1 tbs grated ginger
a splash of soy sauce
4 spring onions
a handful of peanuts

Chicken balls

'Whenever I have any chicken left over from Sunday lunch, I like to concoct these little balls and experiment with different flavours and spices.'

Chop up the chicken finely. Fry onions. Squeeze out water from bread. In a bowl, mix chicken, onion, bread, spices, egg and seasoning. Knead well and shape into small balls or flat patties. Dust with flour and deep-fry for a few minutes until golden. Drain on kitchen paper. A squeeze of lemon enhances the flavour. Sometimes I add a tablespoon of hummus to the mixture and chopped fresh coriander, or mint with a good pinch of chilli powder.

1 cup cooked chicken
2 slices of stale bread,
  soaked in water
1 small onion, finely chopped
1 clove of garlic, crushed
1 tsp ground cumin
1 egg, ½ tsp turmeric
flour

Evita's malva pudding

1 cup sugar, 1 egg
1 tsp smooth apricot jam
1 tbs butter, 2 tsp vinegar
1 cup cake flour
1 tsp bicarbonate of soda
½ cup milk, ½ cup cream

Sauce
1 cup cream, ½ cup sugar
6 tbs butter, ½ cup hot water

Beat together sugar, egg and jam. Melt the butter and add the vinegar. Sift flour, bicarbonate of soda and a good pinch of salt in a bowl. Add milk and cream to egg and sugar mixture and mix. Sift in the flour mixture. Add vinegar and butter mixture and mix well. Pour into a buttered baking dish. Cover with foil and bake in a preheated oven at 180°C for 45 minutes until it is firm and the colour is a rich brown. Combine the sauce ingredients in a pot. Heat slowly until the butter has melted and the sugar has dissolved. Pour the sauce over the pudding as it comes out of the oven. Prick with a fork for sauce to penetrate. Serve, hot or cold, with thick cream.

Jean's mieliebread

'I have refused to acknowledge my sister Bambi Kellermann for years and for very good reasons. But if I preach reconciliation through cuisine, I must practise it. This bread, I know, is a favourite of hers. So when she gets back from Berlin (where I believe she is singing cabaret and doing other very un-Afrikaans things), I will bake a whole loaf for her, leave it at her back door in Paarl, knock and run. She'll know it's from me. It's up to Jean's mieliebread to pave that rocky path!'

500 g self-raising flour
500 ml buttermilk
1 tin whole kernel corn

Mix all ingredients and place in a greased bread tin. Leave in a warm place for about 40 minutes, until it rises. Bake at 200°C for 40 minutes. Test with a sosatie stick to see if cooked. If it comes out clean, the bread is done; if not, leave a little longer. You can also use a bottle of beer instead of the buttermilk.

Apple tart

6 apples
1 tsp sugar
1 cinnamon stick
230 g roll puff pastry
smooth apricot jam

Peel and core apples. Cut 3 into chunks and cook with the sugar and cinnamon to make a purée. Slice other 3 apples into thin wedges and poach until soft. Roll out pastry into a greased tart dish. Bake in preheated oven at 200°C for 10 minutes. Remove from oven. Spoon apple purée over the pastry lining. Arrange cooked apple wedges on top. Spread apricot jam over the top. Return to oven for 20 to 30 minutes and bake until golden.

Orange trifle

Mix yoghurt with cinnamon and cardamom. Soak the Madeira cake (or crushed biscuits) in orange juice and Cointreau.

In 4 glasses, layer the soaked cake, spicy yoghurt and chopped oranges. Repeat several times. Decorate with chopped orange and chocolate – curled or grated.

You could use caramelised oranges instead (p. 51).

1 cup plain Greek yoghurt
½ tsp ground cinnamon
½ tsp ground cardamom
Madeira cake slices or
  Boudoir biscuits
1 soupspoon Cointreau
6 oranges, peeled

Teatime

'Bring back afternoon tea – that great British tradition. It is a relaxing way to entertain, as the preparation and cooking can all be done beforehand – and a lovely way to see people who are not keen on lengthy dinner parties. Once you have set out the tray with teacups and flowers, all you have to do is put on the kettle, petal!'

Crumpets

2 cups cake flour
1 tbs baking powder
2 eggs
4 tbs sugar
1 cup milk
1 tbs melted butter

Sift flour, baking powder and a good pinch of salt into a large bowl. In a separate bowl, beat the eggs and sugar. Add milk and butter and mix well. Make a well in the flour and pour in the egg mixture, stirring to form a smooth batter. Lightly grease a heavy-bottomed pan and drop tablespoons of batter into it. When crumpets form bubbles, turn them over to brown lightly on the other side. Serve with butter, jam and cream.

Adri's scones

2 cups plain flour
2 tsp baking powder
5 tbs butter
1 large egg
¾ cup milk

Sift flour, baking powder and a good pinch of salt into a large bowl. Using your fingers, rub in the butter until mixture is crumbly. Whisk the egg and milk. Add to the flour and mix everything with a wooden spoon. Turn out onto a floured board and knead lightly, not too much. Flatten dough to 3 cm thick. Cut out rounds. Place on a lightly greased baking sheet. Brush the tops with milk and bake on the middle shelf at 210°C for 15 minutes until golden brown and well risen. Now all you need is butter, clotted cream and your preferred jams to enjoy this homely favourite.

Muffins

Sift the flour, baking powder and 2 good pinches of salt into a large bowl. In a separate bowl mix the egg, sugar, milk and melted butter. Sift the dry ingredients into the egg mixture and stir to mix until you have a moist but lumpy dough. Fold in the currants and nuts, but don't stir too much. Spoon into a well-greased 12-cup muffin tray. Bake at 210°C for 20 minutes until well risen and browned.

Variation: Add ½ cup of chopped dried apricots, 3 tbs of chopped pecan nuts and 1 tsp ground cinnamon.

2 cups cake flour
4 tsp baking powder
1 jumbo egg
2 tbs castor sugar
1 cup milk
125 g butter, melted and
   slightly cooked
½ cup currants or raisins
3 tbs chopped walnuts

Macaroons

Whisk the egg whites to form firm peaks. Mix the ground almond and castor sugar. Fold in the firm egg whites. Put teaspoons full of the mixture onto greased baking paper. Bake at 180°C for 10 minutes. Watch carefully. You can flavour the macaroons by adding 1 tsp ground cinnamon or vanilla essence to the mixture.

3 egg whites
150 g ground almonds
200 g castor sugar

Dolce Evita

Shortbread biscuits

115 g butter
55 g sugar
180 g plain flour

Cream the butter and sugar in a bowl until smooth. Work in the flour to make a soft dough. Shape into a ball. Roll out the dough on a floured board to 5 mm thick. Cut into any shape you fancy, using biscuit cutter, or a glass to cut out rounds. Bake on a greased baking sheet in a preheated 160°C oven for about 15 minutes or until the biscuits are lightly golden. Cool on a wire rack.

Variations: Add herbs or spices to the dough, e.g. 1 tbs of finely chopped rosemary or ground cinnamon or ground cumin. You experiment!

Cheesecake

1 packet digestive or Tennis
biscuits, 50 g butter, melted

Filling
500 g smooth cottage cheese
2 tbs sugar, 2 eggs
1 tbs cornflour
1 tsp vanilla essence

Crush biscuits and mix with melted butter. Press down into a well-buttered pie dish (or springform cake tin) with the back of a spoon. Place in fridge for half an hour. Whisk cheese, sugar and beaten eggs together. Add cornflour and whisk. Add vanilla and whisk. Pour mixture into mould over biscuit crust and bake in 180°C oven for 35 minutes.

Prolong baking if centre of cake is still soft. Leave in oven for 10 minutes to cool before removing from mould. Flavours improve with time, so try to keep the cake for 24 hours before eating.

Variation: Mix 3 tbs sugar, 2 tbs water and pips and juice of 2 granadillas. Bring to the boil slowly, allow to cool and pour over the cake.

Yoghurt cake

Place ingredients in a large bowl in the same order as listed. Mix well. Butter a springform cake tin. Pour in mixture. Bake in a 180°C oven for 30 minutes. Test with a skewer. Cover cake with foil and bake for another 15 minutes if still moist inside.

Note: This is like a pound cake and very easy to adapt. You can cut it in half, spread apricot jam on the one side and crème fraîche on the other. Then sandwich together.

Variation: Add 1 tsp ground cinnamon and 2 tbs of dried apricots to the batter and top with walnuts. Or add 1 tbs lemon zest to the batter and top with fresh apple or pear slices, sprinkle with pine nuts. This is one of the easiest cakes to make if friends pop in for tea.

Use the yoghurt pot as your measure.
1 pot Bulgarian yoghurt
1½ pots of sugar
3 pots of cake flour
1 tsp baking powder
3 eggs
½ pot of oil

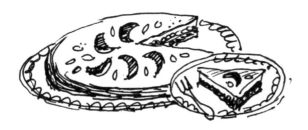

Uda's orange cake

Cream the butter and sugar in a bowl until smooth. Add eggs, flour and baking powder. Mix well. Add zest of 3 oranges and juice of 1 orange. Mix well. Pour batter into a buttered springform cake tin. Bake in a preheated 200°C oven for 15 minutes. Cover with foil. Return to oven and bake for a further 40 minutes at 200°C.

Make the orange sauce. Squeeze juice of 2 oranges and combine with 50 g sugar in a small pot. Heat slowly until sugar is melted. Add a tot of Cointreau if you wish!

Remove cake from the oven and let it cool for a while. Turn out onto a plate while still warm. Prick with a fork and pour over orange sauce. Serve cold. Delicious with vanilla ice cream.

Note: This is a flattish cake, so don't worry if it does not rise.

80 g butter
120 g sugar for cake
3 eggs, 120 g cake flour
½ tbs baking powder
3 oranges
50 g sugar for sauce

Putupap

'Mieliemeal porridge, known as polenta in Italy, is a staple food for many people. Stywepap is very popular at braai parties, especially in the north of the country. It requires patience to make, but can be eaten in many different ways. The classic South African favourite is with gravy, spinach or thick tomato and onion sauce and boerewors.'

Stywepap

4 cups water, 1 tsp salt
2 cups coarse mieliemeal
(traditional braaipap)

Bring salted water to the boil in a large heavy-bottomed pot. Pour in the mieliemeal in a steady stream and stir with a fork. Cover. Reduce heat and simmer for 40 minutes, stirring occasionally. Add another ½ cup of cold water to porridge. Let it simmer over low heat for another 30 minutes.

Cheese squares

Spread goat's cheese or crumble feta over the firm putupap. Cut into long strips or squares. Place in a hot oven and grill until the cheese has melted. In the meantime, toss salad leaves and rocket in a bowl with 2 tbs olive oil and 2 tsp balsamic vinegar and arrange on a serving platter. Place the squares on top.

Krummelpap

2 cups water, 1 tsp salt
3 cups coarse mieliemeal

Bring salted water to the boil in a large heavy-bottomed pot. Add mieliemeal in a steady stream, but don't stir. Cover and simmer for 15 minutes over low heat. Stir with a fork until the pap becomes crumbly. Cover again and simmer for another 20 to 30 minutes.

Press into small balls with your hands and soak up meat sauce.

Polenta

4 cups water, 1 tsp salt
2 cups coarse mieliemeal

Bring salted water to the boil in a heavy-bottomed pot. Sprinkle in the mieliemeal and lower heat. Simmer and stir for 30 minutes. When the spoon stands up on its own and the porridge comes away from the side of the pot, it is cooked. Pour the porridge onto a large wooden board. Spread it out and flatten to 3 cm thick and set aside to cool. Cut into squares or lengths and grill until golden brown on both sides, or fry squares in olive oil in a non-stick pan.

Grilled squares

Grilled squares of putupap are very good with all roasted or grilled poultry in any form – crispy chicken wings with chilli tomato sauce, chicken kebabs or roasted quail. The fat of these mini chickens has a most delicate flavour, especially when roasted, and add style to any dinner party.

Putupap gratin

Roll cooked putupap into small balls. Place in a buttered oven-proof dish. Spoon over tomato and onion sauce. Sprinkle with Parmesan cheese. Bake in a 180°C oven for 20 minutes until sauce is bubbling and cheese is golden.

Variation: Combine cooked spinach and putupap. Make balls with your hands. Pour over some cream and sprinkle with Parmesan cheese. Bake for 20 minutes at 180°C.

Variation: Fry the putupap balls in olive oil and serve with chilli tomato sauce.

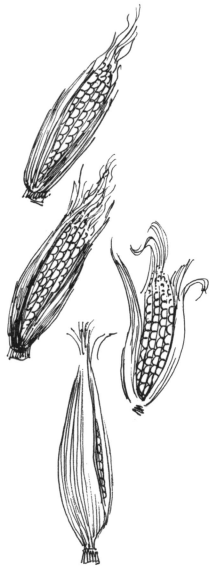

Putu mushroom pie

500 g cooked putupap
2 cups cream
1 cup grated Parmesan cheese
2 tbs butter
1 leek, chopped
500 g mushrooms, sliced
1 tbs chopped parsley

Make the putupap. Pour into a cold large flat dish, spread out to 1.5 cm thick and let it cool. Mix cream and Parmesan. Heat butter and a little oil in a pan. Sauté chopped leek. Add mushrooms and sauté for a few minutes, adding parsley and a little cream. Season. Remove from heat. Cut the cold pap to fit baking dish. Spoon some cream mixture into the dish. Place one half of pap cake on top. Spoon over half the leek and mushroom mixture. Place the other half of the pap cake on top. Spoon over remaining mushroom mixture and spread out evenly. Pour over the rest of the cream and Parmesan. Bake at 180°C for 30 minutes. Serve as a simple lunch with a salad of mixed leaves, vinaigrette and a scattering of cashew nuts.

Mielie muffins

1 cup plain flour
1 tbs baking powder
¼ tsp salt
1 cup fine mieliemeal
1 tbs castor sugar
1 egg
½ cup milk
¼ cup oil
440 g tin whole kernel corn
3 tsp chopped parsley

Coat a 12-hole muffin pan with butter. Sift flour, baking powder and salt into a large bowl. Add the mieliemeal and sugar. Mix well. In a separate bowl, combine egg, milk and oil, drained whole kernel corn and parsley. Add this to the dry mixture. Stir. The batter should be moist and lumpy, so don't over-mix. Preheat oven to 210°C. Spoon mixture into the muffin pan and bake for 20 minutes until golden. Leave to cool on a wire rack before removing muffins.

Try other ingredients – grated carrots, courgettes, cheddar cheese, spices, etc.

Samp & beans (Umngqusho)

Another South African staple food. Soak samp and beans overnight in cold water. Drain. Place in a large pot and cover well with fresh water. Bring to boil, simmer gently, reducing heat, for about 1½ hours until soft. Ensure water doesn't boil away, adding extra if samp and beans dry out. Drain once cooked. Season. Serve hot or cold. I like to add cooked spinach and drizzle olive oil over, and serve with sea salt and black pepper, as well as chunks of feta cheese. In fact, one can add anything one fancies, like tinned tuna or chopped tomatoes and onions.

300 g samp
200 g sugar beans

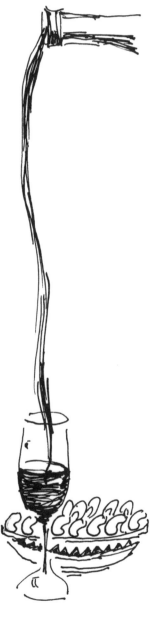

Come for a Braai

'Oom Sampie always had two fires going as he couldn't bear running out of hot coals – one feeding coals to the other. Men love doing this and spend hours stoking up the fire. He gave me some good tips – thick cuts should cook slowly and thin cuts have to be closer to the coals. As chicken takes a long time to braai, it should be parboiled, then braaied to get that lovely smoky flavour.'

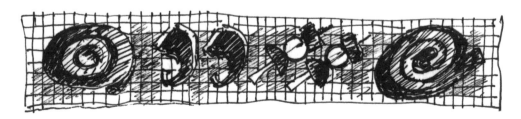

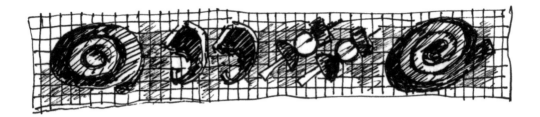

Curry frikkadels

Sauté onion in a little oil until transparent. Add curry powder
and stir for a few minutes over low heat. Add mince. Remove
from heat and stir in the chutney and chilli. When cool, make
flat frikkadels with your hands. Braai over medium-hot coals
until cooked through – about 10 minutes. Delicious with
garlic yoghurt, tomato sauce or chutney. Serve with vetkoek
or puri.

1 onion, chopped
1 tbs curry powder
500 g minced beef, lamb
  or ostrich
1 tbs chutney
1 chilli, chopped

Sosaties

Thread meat onto skewers, alternating lamb cubes, apricots
and onion quarters. Sauté sliced onions and garlic slowly in
oil in a heavy-bottomed pot until transparent. Add the curry
powder and turmeric, stirring. Add sugar, chilli, vinegar
and apricot jam and simmer for about 10 minutes. Remove
from heat to cool. Pour over kebabs and marinate overnight.
Braai over low coals for between 15 and 20 minutes, turning
frequently. You can boil the marinade for a few minutes and
pour over sosaties when serving. Don't forget the putupap for
the gravy.

1 kg shoulder of lamb, cubed
12 dried apricots
2 onions, quartered
2 onions, sliced
1 tbs curry powder
1 tsp turmeric
2 tbs brown sugar
1 red chilli, chopped
1 cup wine vinegar
2 tbs apricot jam
2 cloves of garlic, crushed

Spareribs – lamb or pork

Place all ingredients, except ribs, in a pot and bring to
the boil. Turn down heat and simmer for about 5 minutes.
Remove from heat. Pour over spareribs and marinate overnight. Braai over medium-hot coals for about 20 minutes, or
until cooked through. Baste the ribs frequently.

1 kg lamb or pork spareribs
1 cup rooibos tea
1 cup chutney, 2 tbs oil
½ cup tomato sauce
4 tbs wine vinegar
1 onion, chopped
2 cloves of garlic, crushed
2 tbs honey, 2 tbs soy sauce

Pork kebabs

Cut bacon rashers in half and roll up. Cut up pork and pineapple into cubes. Skewer, alternating bacon, pineapple and pork, repeating three times. Braai over medium-hot coals, turning regularly.

Roosterkoek

400 g cake flour
15 ml baking powder
100 g butter, diced
2 eggs, 150 ml water
50 ml skim milk powder

Sift together flour, baking powder and a good pinch of salt in a bowl. Rub diced butter into the flour with fingertips. Beat eggs and water and add to flour and skim milk powder. Mix well. Knead into a firm, elastic dough. Pull pieces from dough and shape into flat cakes.

Braai over moderate coals, turning frequently, for about 20 minutes.

Chicken kebabs

Marinate chicken breasts in 1 tbs olive oil, 4 tbs soy sauce, 1 tbs curry powder, 1 crushed garlic clove, 2 tbs grated ginger and chopped green chilli for ½ hour. Cut breasts into strips and thread onto kebab sticks which have been soaked in water. Braai for 3 or 4 minutes over moderate coals.

Boerewors

No recipe for boerewors here, but I recommend you buy the best you can. Braai slowly over medium coals in a coil, turning regularly. Keep the juice in the wors, so don't prick!

Steak

Rump, fillet, T-bone, etc. Brush steak with oil and seal over hot coals. Cook for 10 to 12 minutes for rare and 5 to 10 minutes longer for medium. There is nothing like a good steak, cut from well-ripened meat.

Rump steak kebabs

Cut steak into cubes and skewer, alternating meat, pearl onions and green pepper squares. Braai over moderate coals, turning frequently, for 10 to 15 minutes.

Chicken liver sosaties

8 rashers streaky bacon
500 g chicken livers
1 onion, quartered
16 button mushrooms

Separate chicken liver lobes. Cut bacon rashers in half and wrap around each piece of liver. Thread onto skewers – alternating onion chunks, liver and mushrooms, repeating three times. Drizzle with oil. Braai over medium-hot coals, turning a few times until done. Eat with putupap!

Basting

Tie a few rosemary twigs together to make a basting brush. Dip into marinade and baste meat frequently while braaiing. Use sage twigs for pork and fennel fronds for fish.

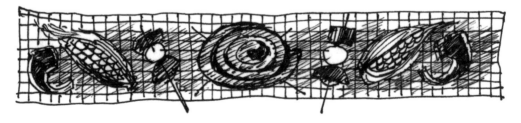

Vetkoek

500 g cake flour
1 tsp baking powder
1 egg, beaten
200 ml milk (or buttermilk)
1 tsp oil

Sift flour, baking powder and a pinch of salt into a large bowl. Mix egg, milk and oil and add to flour. Blend well to make a thickish mixture that drips off the spoon. Deep-fry tablespoonsful in hot oil for a few minutes, turning until golden brown. Drain on kitchen paper. Serve warm.

Lamb frikkadels

Mix 500 g minced lamb with 1 chopped onion, 1 tbs chopped fresh mint, 2 crushed cloves of garlic, a pinch of salt and pepper. Shape into frikkadels with your hands and braai over moderate coals for 10 minutes or until cooked.

Chicken peri-peri

See recipe, Graça's lunch, (p. 60).

Mielies

Fresh mielies are delicious roasted over coals in their leaves, but open up to pull out the silk first. Braai over hot coals for about 20 minutes, turning frequently and brushing with melted butter.

Garlic

Wrap whole garlic bulbs in foil with fresh thyme sprigs and a drizzling of olive oil. Braai over medium coals for about 30 minutes or until soft. Unwrap and squeeze out over fresh bread or toast, with sea salt, or squeeze onto baked potatoes or grilled meat.

Potatoes

Wrap up in foil, together with rosemary sprigs. Sprinkle with salt and olive oil. Place parcels in the coals and cook for about 40 minutes. Sweet potatoes will cook in less time – about 30 minutes.

You can also wrap up butternut chunks in foil, to cook in 30 minutes.

Pork chops

Marinate chops for 1 hour in 1 tbs olive oil, 2 tbs soy sauce, 1 tbs grated ginger, 3 crushed cloves of garlic and 1 tsp lemon zest. Drain. Slash the fat and braai over moderate coals, basting with marinade, for about 15 minutes.

Ostrich patties

Mix 500 g minced ostrich, 1 chopped onion, 1 chopped green chilli, 1 tsp ground cumin, salt and pepper. Mix well using a fork. Form patties with your hands and braai over moderate coals for about 10 minutes.

Putupap squares

See recipes on p. 86 on how to cook. Once cooked, spread the putupap on a wooden board and flatten to 3 cm thick. When cool, cut into thick squares and braai until crispy. Delicious with boerewors, frikkadels and chilli tomato sauce.

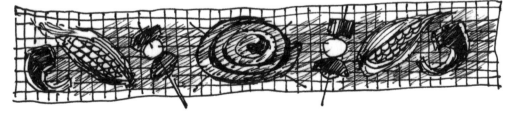

93

Fish Braai

'It's best to braai fish like kabeljou, Cape salmon, steenbras, etc. whole, in a fish basket over a coolish fire. Snoek is "vlekked", then braaied open, skin-side down, on an oiled, hinged grid over moderate coals for about 20 minutes, basting with lemon butter. Turn over to brown quickly for a few minutes – too long will dry out the flesh. Serve with whole sweet potatoes that have been baked in foil amongst the coals.'

Kingklip kebabs

Cut kingklip into cubes. Marinate for an hour in ½ cup of white wine, ½ cup of olive oil, a bunch of fresh fennel fronds, cut up, and 1 tsp fennel seeds.

Thread onto skewers, alternating chunks of deseeded cucumber and kingklip. Braai over medium coals, turning, until cooked through.

Crayfish

Delicious braaied on the beach immediately after being caught. Split the crayfish in two by inserting a knife into the head and cutting it in half. Place on grid over medium coals, flesh-side down, for about 3 minutes only. Turn and baste with butter. Cook for a further 12 minutes or so.

Harders

Wrap harders individually in green vine leaves that have been blanched in hot water – Mediterranean style. Braai over medium coals, 3 minutes each side. When you peel off the vine leaf, it removes the skin at the same time.

Whole kabeljou

Make a stuffing. Chop onion finely and place in a bowl, adding 1 tbs chopped parsley, a pinch of oregano, 1 tbs chopped olives, 1 tsp capers, 2 crushed cloves of garlic, 1 tbs olive oil, salt and pepper. Mix together and stuff into cavity of fish. Place whole fish in a fish basket and braai over medium coals for 20 minutes until skin blisters and browns. Serve with potatoes baked in foil in the coals.

Skottel Braai

'Easy to prepare and quick to cook. A skottel can be taken on picnics – so easy to pack – with a gas bottle – for a brunch fry-up on the beach or in the bush. It's also great for informal home entertaining. Very healthy too. Make different stir-fry sauces to add halfway through cooking. Here are some basic recipes. You can add any vegetable or meat you fancy, as long as everything has been cut into thin strips, slices or cubes for quick cooking.'

Noodle stir-fry

300 g Chinese noodles
4 spring onions, chopped
2 chicken breasts, thinly sliced, or
    300 g pork loin, thinly sliced
½ Chinese cabbage
6 medium broccoli florets, sliced
2 tbs soy sauce
a dash of sherry

Place noodles in boiling water in a skottel and boil for 5 minutes. Drain and rinse in cold water. Heat 2 tbs peanut oil in the skottel. Add spring onions and chicken and stir-fry for a minute. Add noodles and stir-fry for 3 minutes. Add shredded cabbage, broccoli, soy sauce and a dash of sherry and stir-fry for a further 5 minutes, until cooked through. If necessary, add a dash of water to moisten, and a squeeze of lemon.

Chicken with nuts

2 dried red chillies
500 g chicken breasts, cut into strips
2 tbs peanuts or cashews

Sauce for stir-fry
2 tbs chicken stock, 2 tbs dry sherry
1 tbs soy sauce, 2 tbs cider vinegar
2 tsp sugar, 1 tbs chopped garlic
1 tbs chopped spring onions
1 tsp grated root ginger

Heat 3 tbs peanut oil in a skottel. Add dried chillies, cut in half lengthwise, and stir-fry for a few seconds. Add chicken strips and the nuts and fry for a minute or two. Remove everything from the skottle. Place sauce ingredients in the skottel and bring to the boil. Lower heat and return chicken and nuts to the skottel and cook for a further 5 minutes. Garnish with chopped spring onions.

Potjiekos

'Potjiekos requires long, slow cooking. Oom Sampie's idea of having two fires going makes perfect sense, as coals have to be added to the potjie fire from time to time, to keep it simmering over low heat. Meat cuts like neck, chuck, shin of beef, lamb shanks, pork breast, oxtail, venison and guinea fowl are ideally suited to potjiekos as the long cooking process tenderises the meat. Firm, fresh vegetables added to this make for a wonderfully tasty meal. The idea is to arrange the ingredients in layers. First brown the meat in oil in the potjie you've placed over hot coals. Vegetables that require longer cooking are placed at the bottom, while faster-cooking vegetables like courgettes are placed on top. Put the lid on the potjie and do not stir. Once the pot starts bubbling after an hour or two, you can open the pot and prick the vegetables on top. If they are soft, the potjie should be ready. While the potjie is gently bubbling away, you have time to "gesels" and make the traditional accompaniments – vetkoek (p. 93), mieliebread (p. 80), putupap (p. 86), pampoenkoekies (pumpkin fritters) (p. 29), etc. and prepare this fabulous party surprise – pampoenpot!'

Pampoenpot à la Gerber

1 crown pumpkin
1 tin condensed milk
1 packet Safari fruit cake mix

Line a potjie with tinfoil. Cut lid off pumpkin and take out the pips. Rub pumpkin with oil. Fill with fruit cake mix and pour over condensed milk. Replace pumpkin lid and wrap whole pumpkin in foil. Place in potjie and cover with pot lid. Heap coals on top and around the sides of the potjie. Cook for about 2 hours. Eat as an accompaniment. This is a great party trick!

Oom Rudolf's potjie

Chop vegetables. Heat oil in a potjie over hot coals. Season meat and brown on all sides. Add onions, garlic and a sprig of thyme (or any herb you fancy). Sauté until transparent. Add vegetables and 2 cups of hot water. Stir carefully to combine. Replace lid. Cook until vegetables are almost soft – about 45 minutes. Mix in 1 cup of beef stock (the packet of oxtail soup powder with 1 cup of boiling water). Carefully stir into ingredients, adding whole kernel corn. Leave pot to simmer – listening to the gentle bubbling – until vegetables are soft. Serve with rice or putupap (p. 86).

4 medium potatoes
4 carrots, 2 large onions
2 cups green beans
4 pieces beef shin or neck, or
   2 kg lamb knuckles or neck
2 cloves of garlic
herbs to taste
1 packet oxtail soup
1 tin whole kernel corn,
   drained

Curry potjie

Follow the above recipe, but once the onions are transparent, add garlic, ginger, cardamom, cinnamon stick, turmeric, chilli and meat masala. Mix well. Add 2 chopped tomatoes. Cover and simmer for 45 minutes. Add vegetables and simmer for a further 45 minutes.

The ultimate tomato bredie

Follow the above recipe, but once the onions have been sautéed, add 6 large, ripe tomatoes, skinned and diced. Season. Add 1 cup of heated meat stock and 2 tsp sugar. Cover and simmer for 1 hour until meat is tender. Add 4 quartered potatoes and a little extra stock and simmer for another 30 minutes. When potatoes are cooked, stir very gently and serve with rice, but stywepap (p. 86) is ideal to go with this flavourful tomato sauce.

Store Cupboard Cooking

'When people suddenly pop in for a drink or tea, I look to the store cupboard (freezer or pantry). I need to make a quick appetiser (never drink on an empty stomach) or something sweet for tea. See that your store cupboard is well stocked (you never know ...) with tins of beans, chickpeas, sweetcorn, tuna, sardines, cherries, tinned tomatoes, dry pasta, lentils, rice, mieliemeal, samp, flour, onions, frozen puff pastry, peas and spinach. Keep stale bread to make Melba toast or breadcrumbs for stuffings, or rissoles. Stale baguette is perfect for herb toasts. I must thank my dear mother Ouma Ossewania for this tip.'

Pea Salad

250 g frozen peas
2 tbs mayonnaise, 2 tbs sour cream
2 spring onions, finely chopped
1 tbs chopped mint

I always have frozen peas in the freezer – petit pois. They come in handy for adding to so many dishes – like curries, rice, pasta – or to make this salad.

Cook peas in boiling water for 4 minutes. Drain. Mix mayonnaise and sour cream with chopped spring onions and mint and season. Spoon onto whole salad leaves, like chicory or butter lettuce.

Chickpea salad & pasta

Drain and rinse chickpeas. Chop 1 medium onion and sauté slowly in olive oil until transparent, adding 1 tsp of ground cumin. Add 1 crushed garlic clove, chickpeas, salt and pepper and a splash of good vinegar. Stir to combine. A delicious snack! If your friends are really hungry, reach for that packet of spaghetti – 100 g per person – and cook to al dente. Add to the pan with chickpeas, toss well and serve at once.

Hummus

Once you have cooked the chickpeas as above, place in a bowl and, using a fork, mash to make a rough paste (or liquidise to make a smooth purée). Add extra olive oil and lemon juice and season. Add Tabasco for a hot taste. Serve with herb toasts.

Butter beans & tuna

Follow the same recipe as for chickpea salad, but use butter beans, cut 2 onions into rings for sautéing and add oregano. Open a tin of tuna and spoon onto salad. Top with quartered hard-boiled eggs.

Herb toasts

Cut a day-old baguette into thin slices. Place on a baking tray. Sprinkle with a little oil and herbes de Provence (a mixture of dried herbs). Grill for a minute (or two). Do not leave unattended – they brown very quickly. Remove when golden and sprinkle with salt and pepper. Serve toasts with hummus, or on their own.

Toasted sardines

Drain tinned sardines. Mash with a fork. Add 1 tsp of chopped capers, 1 tsp finely chopped onion and a squeeze of lemon. Spread on slices of day-old bread or baguette. Place under a hot grill for 2 minutes or until bread is toasted. Watch carefully to prevent burning.

Clafoutis

2 eggs, 125 g plain flour
1 cup milk, 3 tbs sugar
450 g jar of cherries

Butter a pie dish. Mix eggs, flour, milk, a pinch of salt and 1 tbs sugar. Drain cherries and put into an ovenproof dish. Pour the batter over the cherries. Bake for about 40 minutes at 180°C. Remove from oven, sprinkle the rest of the sugar over and return to oven for 5 to 10 minutes.

Cinnamon toast

bread, 5 tbs butter
3 tsp brown sugar
3 tsp ground cinnamon

Cut several slices of bread, toast and remove crusts. Soften butter and mix in the sugar and cinnamon. Spread onto the hot toast. Make a pile of toast, keep warm and cut into fingers when ready to serve.

Beautifully Preserved

'Ouma Ossewania's kitchen was her throne – there she reigned supreme, dictating what everyone ate. Very powerful indeed, but only temporarily, as I soon learnt to cook. She used to buy fruit and vegetables in bulk at the market (always very economical) and then spent a day or 2 pickling and preserving. Bambi and I loved all the activity in the kitchen when we were kids, but used to fight a lot as we licked out the preserving pan. "Moenie laf wees nie!" Ouma used to say. "There's enough for the whole dorp – just look at all those jars." The beautiful and colourful preserves lining the shelves in the pantry were her pride and joy and we always had presents to give away at any time.

In these stressful times, I find it very comforting and rewarding to put a day aside to make my own preserves and think of the good old days when Ouma was still *compos mentis*. Here are a few favourites.'

Sterilizing jars

Either boil in a large pot for 10 minutes – lids too – and dry by placing on a kitchen paper-lined tray in oven at 100°C. Or wash jars, place on a kitchen paper-lined tray and then in a 160°C oven for 10 minutes. Cool before filling the jars. To seal, cover the preserve with a wax paper disk, or cover with clingwrap – then screw on the lid, or tie with elastic band.

Apple chutney

1 kg Granny Smith apples
2 large onions, chopped
2 red chillies, chopped
2 cups brown sugar
1 cup sultanas
2 tbs chopped ginger
1 tsp sea salt
3 whole cloves
2 cups cider vinegar

Peel, core and chop the apples. Gently cook ingredients in a large heavy pot until mixture thickens – about 40 minutes, stirring occasionally. Ladle into jars. Seal when cool.

Chilli herb oil

3 cups olive oil
6 bird's eye chillies
 a good pinch of oregano
2 sprigs of dry thyme

Place all dry ingredients into an attractive bottle. Pour over olive oil and seal. Leave for 2 weeks to infuse.

Boeremeisies

Make syrup using 1 cup of sugar and 2 cups of water. Add 10 fresh, whole apricots. Turn off heat. Add 1 cup of brandy. Place in sterilized jars and seal. Delicious with vanilla ice cream.

Blatjang

Soak 500 g dried apricots in water for 2 hours. Boil in a little of this water until soft. Mash into a rough purée. Add 2 cloves, crushed garlic and 1 tsp chilli powder and salt. Mix thoroughly and add 1 cup of red wine vinegar. Pour into jars. Use as a condiment with curry or meat – or snoek.

Dried tomatoes

1 kg ripe Roma tomatoes
4 tbs sea salt
1 tbs oregano, bay leaves
black peppercorns
olive oil to fill jars

Cut tomatoes in half and remove seeds. Place the halves, cut side up, on a baking tray lined with parchment paper. Sprinkle with salt and oregano. Place in a preheated 100°C oven overnight or for about 10 hours. When tomatoes are dry and cool, pack them into sterilized jars, adding a bay leaf or two and a few peppercorns, cover with olive oil and seal. Store in a cool, dark place for 2 months. On a very hot day, you can dry tomatoes in the sun.

Apricot jam

1 kg fresh apricots
4 tbs water
2½ cups sugar
juice of 1 lemon
2 tbs Grand Marnier

Cut apricots in half and remove pips. Place in a heavy-bottomed pot with a little water, sugar and lemon juice and simmer until fruit is soft. Stir now and then until sugar has dissolved. Then boil mixture until it is thick enough to coat a spoon. Stir in Grand Marnier. Let it cool. Pour jam into sterilized jars and seal. Try this using dried apricots, soaked overnight.

A Weekend in Darling

'Our beautiful town is less than an hour's drive from Cape Town. I can thoroughly recommend visiting us, and at any time of the year, too – not just to come to one of my shows, but to enjoy the area and all it has to offer.

The annual Wildflower Show in spring has been an event since 1917. Nothing can match the beauty of our wildflowers – the colours in the veld will send shivers down your spine – along with the Duckitts' Orchid Show and the Voorkamerfees. There is so much to do – birdwatching, a wildflower walk, game drives, wine tasting, museums and art galleries, great restaurants and coffee shops, B&Bs – and don't forget about the golf course!

But first you should have breakfast at The Perron.'

Station Breakfast

'Our station breakfast is fit for a queen – a delicious mixture of melt-in-the-mouth tastes: 2 eggs, 2 boerewors, 2 bacon slices and tomato, 2 slices of toast, butter and jam, tea or coffee. Kiddies breakfast is the same, but half the quantity with orange juice. If you're not hungry, try our muffins – then go for a stroll around the dorp.'

Gorgeous gay muffins

Sift together the dry ingredients. Mix the egg and buttermilk and the melted butter. Beat and then add to dry ingredients. Mix lightly, then spoon into a well-greased 12-cup muffin pan. Bake in the oven at 220°C for 15 to 20 minutes.

Serve with grated Cheddar cheese and jam.

1 cup cake flour
1 cup wholewheat flour
4 tbs baking powder
2 tbs sugar, ½ tsp salt
1 egg, beaten
1 cup buttermilk
4 tbs melted butter

Wuppertal wonderfill

We serve the Cederberg's magic tea – rooibos, another national treasure. We use it in our soups, sauces, stews and cakes instead of water. It is full of minerals and nutrients to keep you healthy. I recommend that you drink it black to relieve indigestion or a hangover, or to make a delicious iced tea for those hot Darling days, *wanneer die kraaie gaap ...*

Iced rooibos tea

Boil water. Add the tea bags and sugar. Allow to infuse for 10 minutes. Remove tea bags and leave to cool. Fill a jug with ice and pour in the cold tea. Add the freshly squeezed orange juice and 1 tbs of lemon juice. Add orange and lemon slices and fresh mint. Stir well and serve in glasses. This is a good drink to serve to your diabetic friends, as it tastes like a cocktail.

1 *l* boiling water
4 rooibos tea bags
2 tbs castor sugar
1 cup fresh orange juice or
    fruit juice of choice
1 tbs lemon juice
½ orange, sliced
½ lemon, sliced
6 sprigs fresh mint

Welcome to Evita se Perron!

'When I saw it for the first time in 1995, the former railway station was a deserted little blik-building in an expanse of useless gravel and stifling dust. It was nothing but an old derelict station that no train would ever be able to use again. The local carpenter was working from there, and as he was repairing shutters at the Old Age Home, I was out on a visit, bringing him a *boereraat* for his migraine.

I stood under the palm trees on the station verandah, the railway lines glistening like mercury in the sun. Then, suddenly, the words flashed (like mercury!) into my head: *Evita se Perron*. It made so much sense. Of course I had in mind Eva Perón, that woman from Argentina who sang all those songs and then died. I am also fondly called Evita, of course, and "Perron", you see, is the Afrikaans word for a station platform.

So we started the whole business with a small stage and twelve tables for lunch on Sundays. It worked. We then extended into a new building, inspired by the same blik architecture and strange colour-scheme that we had inherited. It seems the station building was so rusty that the few people who truly wanted to save the building each brought a tin of paint from the garage. One brought a tin of pink paint, someone else brought green, another blue – and nowadays these are our international colours.

Goods trains rattle past every hour on the hour, causing everything to shake and shudder, including the six cats, who are as precious to us as our audiences. People sometimes come to the Perron just to hug the cats.

Our plans for the future include cameras in our venue, so that if a guest of note arrives, I can do an interview on camera, which we can quickly edit and send on to *YouTube*, *Facebook*, *UpMine* and *InYours* within minutes.

The future is here, and we will not be shy to annex it!

We also have a collection of apartheid artefacts and symbols: signs, flags, photos and letters that remind us of who were a part of that era, and how lucky we are to be rid of it … and to make sure that those who are too young – thank goodness – to recognise the pain, will take care that such meanness never happens again. I call it a Museum; De Kock calls it a Nauseum.

So Darling Station is now home to the world's most extraordinary memory of a bad past, as well as being an inspiration for a great future.'

Evita's homemade bread

Mix together dry ingredients in a bowl. Pour in the beer and mix well, using a sharp knife. Pour into a well-greased loaf tin. Bake at 180°C for an hour. Turn out on a rack to cool. For a larger loaf, double the quantities. You can also bake it in a black pot. Why not experiment with different ingredients, like sprinkling sesame seeds over the top, or cumin powder instead of mixed herbs?

500 g self-raising flour
1 tsp salt
1 tbs sugar
2 tsp mixed herbs
340 ml beer

The Perron snack platter

biscuits
cherry tomatoes
cocktail gherkins
pickled onions
cheese strips
savoury dip
sugar-snap peas
biltong
droëwors
minibutters
boiled eggs

Jan van Riebeeck infusion

2 cinnamon sticks
1 tbs chopped ginger
8 cardamom pods
4 whole cloves
4 tbs sugar
4 tea bags
1 tbs lemon juice
½ lemon, sliced

They told us that Jan van Riebeeck brought civilization to South Africa on 6th April 1652. How could he? He was from Holland! Now we know the truth: Jan van Riebeeck was an escaped Dutch convict that came to steal chickens from the Bushmen!

A delicious tea to end off a meal, or to serve on a Cape of Storms winter afternoon. Bring 1 litre water to the boil with cinnamon, fresh ginger, cardamom, cloves and sugar. Cover, lower heat and simmer for 10 minutes. Add the tea bags, lemon juice and lemon slices and steep for 3 minutes. Strain and pour into glasses. Add sugar to taste.

Ouma Ossewania's brandewynkoek

250 g dates, chopped
1 tsp bicarbonate of soda
1 cup boiling water
125 g butter, 1 cup sugar
2 eggs, beaten
2 cups flour
1 tsp baking powder
1 cup chopped walnuts

Sauce
1 cup sugar, 1 tsp butter
150 ml water, ½ cup brandy
1 tsp vanilla essence

Place half the dates in a bowl. Mix bicarbonate of soda into the boiling water and pour over. Mix well and leave to cool. Cream the butter and sugar. Add beaten eggs and mix well. Sift in flour, a good pinch of salt and baking powder. Add rest of the dry dates with the nuts and blend well. Stir in the date and bicarbonate of soda mixture and mix well. Pour batter into a well-greased baking dish. Bake at 180°C for about 40 minutes. While this is in the oven, prepare the sauce. Heat the sugar, butter and water over medium heat for around 5 minutes. Remove from the heat and stir in the brandy, vanilla essence and a good pinch of salt. Pour the syrup over the pudding while it is still hot. This is Ouma's treat – hot or cold – with cream of any kind.

Tannie's melktert

'When I was a little girl at school in Bethlehem in the Orange Free State, I remember how traumatised I was by that picture of the Battle of Blood River that hung on the wall next to my table (I was in Standard Four for 2 years because I'd broken my leg and a snake bit me – twice). Those images of violence and bloodletting were enough to drive me, as a young Christian Afrikaans girl, quite insane. I voted for the NP! No wonder so many of us Afrikaners are so deeply disturbed. And then I was introduced to melktert. It was soft on my pain, candy floss against my fears. Melktert is more than milk and less of a tart. It is that kiss of life from one who knows life to one who needs love. Melktert is the cushion after the traumatic fall from Hell, the duvet of warmth after the avalanche of guilt has frozen your soul. Melktert is the ultimate weapon of sweet destruction. Hand a piece of melktert to the person who confronts you with a gun. You will end up with that gun, leaving the antagonist with another few kilos on his hips.'

Roll out puff pastry and use it to line a greased pie dish. Bake blind for 10 minutes at 180°C. Heat two-thirds of the milk and butter over low heat to just below boiling point. Set aside. Beat the sugar, cornflour, egg yolks, the rest of the milk and the vanilla essence and add this mixture to the hot milk. Beat the egg whites until stiff. Beat the custard mixture and add to the hot milk. Fold in egg whites carefully. Pour the mixture into the pastry case, sprinkle with ground cinnamon and bake at 180°C for 30 minutes or until the filling has set.

250 g puff pastry
  (buy a good one)
300 ml milk
75 g butter
100 g sugar
30 ml cornflour
2 eggs, separated
1 tsp vanilla essence

Meet Me at the Perron!

'What brought me to Darling? (Besides the fact that in Afrikaans the name translates as "Skattie"?) My mother, Ouma Ossewania Kakebenia Poggenpoel, who was born during the Anglo-Boer War (so work out how old she is and don't tell her) lives in the Groeneweide Old Age Home in Darling. It is the only one left in South Africa who will take her, because my mother insists on having a braaivleis in her room every Friday afternoon. She has burnt down 17 old age homes. The one in Darling has agreed to stand by with hoses on Fridays because I pay them in dollars (American, not Zimbabwean).

Then I got to know the town and its people. Darling is a busy town, a working town. Not a tourist fossil like Franschhoek, or a botox warehouse like Plett. Darling works and earns and lives and smiles. That's what I love about it more than anything. The glass in Darling is always half-full, never half-empty. And it is that sense of hope and adventure that inspired me to ask my dear friend Linda to help me compile this beautiful book.

When I say "Meet me at the Perron", it is possible. I try and be there every weekend and invite you to have lunch and dinner, to sample the culinary treasures you have discovered in this book. I will also get onto the little stage and encourage you to rethink your fears. To laugh at that fear and so make it less fearful. And to realise that it is not politically or socially incorrect to spend time in the kitchen and cook for those you love. Of course, cooking for those you loathe might change the future of the world. Get enemies together and watch them eat, drink and be merry. Who can fight when you're chewing your favourite treat?

Visit www.evita.co.za for more information. '

Thabo's renaissance crumble

'Our former President is going through a difficult time, now that they refer to his government as the "former regime". (What a relief! They used to call us old Nats that!) Thabo, the intellectual, would make such wonderful speeches. I never knew what he meant, but he would quote from Shakespeare, Woolworths and Thesaurus. (Does he know the name Thabo is an anagram for the name Botha?)'

Make the crumble first. Mix the flour, butter, egg yolk and a good pinch of salt with your fingers to make a crumbly dough. Put aside to cool.

Prepare a ratatouille: cut all the vegetables up into small chunks. Peel the tomatoes. Cut into chunks, removing the seeds. Heat oil in a large pan and sauté each vegetable separately, until cooked, then combine in a bowl. In the same pan and oil, sauté the onion and garlic. Add the tomatoes, thyme and all other cooked vegetables. Season and simmer over very low heat for 15 minutes without covering. In the meantime, put the cheese, cream and olive oil in a pot and heat gently for 3 minutes, stirring. Season. Spoon the ratatouille into an ovenproof gratin dish. Pour the cream cheese sauce over. Cover with the crumble and bake in a preheated oven at 180°C for 15 to 20 minutes until golden. Serve hot from the gratin dish. Open a bottle of Groote Poste Sauvignon Blanc and mourn the renaissance that should have been.

1 aubergine
3 small courgettes
2 red peppers
3 ripe tomatoes
2 cloves of garlic
1 onion, chopped
sprigs of thyme
1 cup olive oil
120 g cottage cheese
½ cup cream

Crumble
200 g flour
100 g soft butter
1 egg yolk

Bad Taste

'Bad politics do leave a bad taste and even more serious damage. Parliament as usual celebrates the best and vomits up the worst. Tony Yengeni, once ANC Whip in the House, went to prison for fraud and then came out still in his Armani and Gucci, a farce to be reckoned with. Shabir Shaik, financial advisor to Jacob Zuma, was jailed for a cluster of reasons but ill health earned him a parole. He was dying to get out and has proved to be a medical miracle. De Kock saw him eating crayfish in one of Durban's best restaurants recently.'

Yengeni's Swiss chard with 4x4 gravy

a bunch of Swiss chard
50 g butter
30 g flour
1½ cups of chicken stock
1 cup mushrooms, sliced
1 cup diced ham
½ cup cream
parsley

Remove green parts of the chard and use as spinach in another dish. Break the white stalks and remove stringy parts. Cut into pieces and cook in salted, boiling water for 15 minutes. Drain, transfer to a serving dish. While the stalks are cooking, make the 4×4 gravy. Melt the butter in a pan, add flour and stir slowly to combine with chicken stock to make a smooth sauce. Add the mushrooms, diced ham and cream. Pour over the chard stalks. Season and sprinkle over parsley. Serve immediately. Can also be served as a gratin, in which case sprinkle with Parmesan cheese and place under the grill until golden and bubbling.

Shabir's gold coin fricassee

1 chicken
2 tbs chicken fat
600 g carrots
1 tsp ground ginger
2 tbs sultanas
1 cup fresh orange juice
1 tbs sugar
½ cup double cream

Cut the chicken into medium-sized pieces. Season. Sauté in chicken fat or oil until golden. Cut the carrots into thickish rounds (to resemble the gold coins) and add these to the pot, with ginger and sultanas. Add orange juice. Sprinkle the sugar on top. Cover the pan and simmer gently for 30 minutes. Add the double cream and mix in well over low heat to thicken the sauce. Season. Sprinkle with chopped parsley or fresh coriander. Serve hot with boiled potatoes or white rice.

Winnie's Stompie ragout

'I will not join the rush to condemn an extremely elegant, brave and frightening woman, who made those of us then in a powerful National Party Government look and feel like amateurs while she straddled the world as "mother of the nation". Then she took a wrong turning and ended up in the cesspool of bad media. I was as terrified of her as the next Nationalist during those old days. But as I grew out of my shell of fear, I realised that we did really bad things to this wife and mother. Today I watch her from afar and I admire her in spite of my prejudices. And hope that she will never be President, because then she could solve all our problems with a gunshot. Or simply a soccer game.'

Use large brown mushrooms or white button mushrooms, or both. Sauté in a mixture of butter and oil. Add a small glass of marsala or sherry and ½ cup of thick cream. Reduce over low heat until thick and creamy. Sprinkle with chopped parsley and lots of black pepper. Serve as an appetiser with toast, as a garnish for sautéed chicken or fish, or over boiled potatoes for vegetarians.

500 g mushrooms
1 tbs butter
1 small glass of sherry
½ cup thick cream
parsley

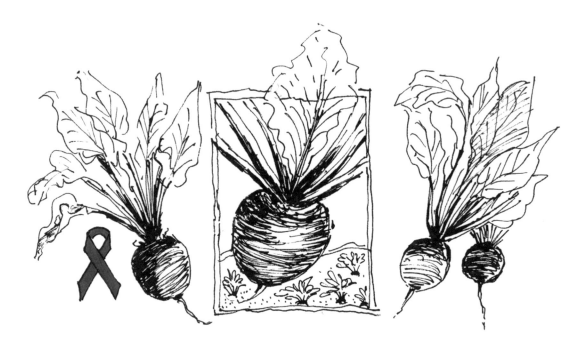

Manto's Mantra

'I have never had a problem with ministers in our government, not even when they were in bed with me. My husband, Hasie, was the Minister of Water Affairs and Minister of Black Housing in HF Verwoerd's government. My Hasie even combined his portfolios by building a black township in a dam! But when De Kock explained to me that a former Minister of Health was the Angel of Death herself, fully disguised and, with a beetroot in one hand, waving around garlic fumes with her tail, I simply had to take note. I also met this woman, Manto Tshabalala-Msimang, and I rather liked her. So until this day I don't know what to think about what they say she recommended using against a terrible virus. It sounds quite ridiculous. But even so, you really shouldn't put all the blame on an innocent little old beetroot or a gnarled piece of garlic!'

Betty's borscht

800 g beetroot, stalks removed
5 cups good chicken stock
1 cup sour cream
1 tbs lemon juice
1 tbs sugar
6 boiled potatoes, peeled

Place the beetroot in a large pot, and cover with boiling water. Add salt. Simmer gently for 40 minutes until tender. Drain and cool. Rub off skins, cut into cubes and return to the large pot. Add chicken stock. Cover and simmer gently for 20 minutes. Transfer beetroot chunks and soup stock to a liquidiser and blend, adding 5 tbs of sour cream. Return to the pot. Add the lemon juice and sugar, and salt and pepper to taste. Reheat, but don't boil. Serve in soup bowls with a boiled potato in each bowl. Swirl in extra sour cream and sprinkle with copped chives. This soup is also delicious cold.

Boesak's Babble & Squeak

'The Reverend Alan Boesak will be remembered as a voice in the wilderness of the struggle against the desert of our apartheid era. Even when he was still my enemy, I listened to him, and appreciated his subversive words in Afrikaans. Then "struggle bookkeeping" got in the way, and Alan went to jail for fraud, maybe following Nelson Mandela's example: that politicians first go to jail before they venture into politics, and not the other way around! Today he is back on his moral high ground, just above his own ego, and still can speak to make crows fall out of trees! And hopefully move on.'

This dish is an important one for leftovers! Potatoes must be cooked and cold. Use leftover spinach or cabbage or cook from scratch. Heat a tablespoon of oil in a large frying pan and fry chopped onion over medium heat until transparent. Finely chop the potato. Combine in a bowl with the onion, greens, salt and pepper. Heat another 2 tbs oil or duck fat in the pan over low heat. Spread the bubble mixture over the base. Fry for 20 minutes or so, turning from time to time when the underside turns golden. Drizzle over extra oil halfway through cooking if necessary. This is a delicious green and golden crispy, lumpy, messy hash. Boesak bo!

olive oil or duck fat
1 large onion, chopped
600 g boiled potatoes
handful or 2 of sliced
   greens (spinach
   or cabbage)

SABC modderkoekies

'What can I say about our public broadcaster? During our time in power it worked for us and now it works for them. Call it the SANC.'

Melt the chocolate and butter in a pot over very low heat. Stir until smooth. Beat the eggs and sugar in a bowl until pale and thick. Fold in the chocolate mixture. Combine the flour and baking powder. Sift this into the mixture. Add the nuts and currants and mix well. Line a square 20 cm baking tin with baking paper. Pour in the mixture and bake at 180°C for 30 minutes. Prick with a skewer to test whether the cake is set. Allow to cool. Cut into squares. Don't worry if they do not cut perfectly. They may look like a battered SABC gemors, but they will still taste delicious! (About 12 square cakes.)

125 g dark chocolate
125 g butter
2 eggs
1 cup of castor sugar
1 heaped cup flour
1 tsp baking powder
1 cup coarsely chopped
   walnuts
½ cup currants

De Kock's Raspberries

'We're bruised and battered thanks to arrogance, corruption, incompetence and plain lack of common sense, says De Kock. He came up with this coulis as we're not too sure as to who or what is worse. Here are a few recipes – you decide who gets the raspberry, which brings me to Dr Koornhof. Liewe Piet. He was such a good friend. And he did so much for South Africa. After being second in command to PW Botha, a true architect of apartheid, Piet Promises proved to the world that Afrikaners could adapt. He lived with a lovely lady of colour and they had a cluster of little brown children. (Barack-Obama-Beige!) When I asked him if he was truly the father of these little treasures, Piet laughed, waggled his big ears and said: "Ja-nee!" Stoute kabouter!'

Raspberry fool

Bruise the raspberries, then press them through a fine sieve.
Mix with sugar and orange-blossom water. Beat the fruit pulp
and cream together until well mixed. Spoon the fool into
glasses and decorate with whole fresh raspberries. You can
use strawberries as well.

4 cups raspberries
1 cup castor sugar
1 tbs orange-blossom water
3 cups cream
berries for decoration

Raspberry coulis

Place fruit in a small pot with sugar and 1 tbs water. Simmer
gently until fruit has disintegrated, stirring from time to time.
Add lemon juice to taste. Spoon over sweet melon, or over
vanilla or chocolate ice cream and decorate with a sprig of
fresh mint.

Why not plant your own raspberry bush – they grow like
weeds and will give you lots of fruit in late summer?

350 g ripe raspberries
100 g castor sugar
1 tsp lemon juice

Laagerfontein Hotel mess

Place gooseberries in a pot over very gentle heat. Cover and
simmer until berries are soft and mushy. Cool. Spoon over
crushed meringue and top with a spoonful or 2 of whipped
cream. Use yoghurt for a less rich dessert.

350 g Cape gooseberries
50 g castor sugar
4 large meringues
1 cup whipped cream or
  Greek yoghurt

Koornhof's Cape Coloured surprise

Alternate scoops of chocolate, caramel and vanilla ice cream
into 4 tall glasses. Spoon the raspberry coulis over the top.
Cover with a spoon or two of whipped cream. Grate dark
chocolate over cream and serve at once.

Of course you can make this surprise with any flavour
you like.

Try making a 'Rainbow Nation': sprinkle hundreds and
thousands or vermicelli on top. Alternate scoops of strawberry,
blueberry, pistachio, lemon or chocolate ice cream – create
your own surprises!

1 cup dark chocolate
  ice cream
1 cup caramel ice cream
1 cup vanilla ice cream
raspberry coulis
1 cup whipped cream
dark chocolate to grate
  on top

Let's go Winetasting!

‘On the road to Darling you'll see blue cranes in the wheat fields, the Nguni holy cows grazing, pelicans flying overhead on their way to Dassen Island, lots of other birdlife, and magnificent flowers if you happen to come during springtime. Be careful on the road – you may inadvertently flatten a tortoise (in the past I would have made tortoise stew to go with Oom Piet's Shiraz, but those days are over). And remember: don't drink and drive. A glass or two of red wine is good for you, but too much alcohol poses a threat to your health.’

'Stop over at Groote Post Wine Estate to taste their marvellous wines and buy a few bottles. Also visit Cloof, Alexanderfontein, Tukula and Darling Cellars. We are so proud of the wonderful wine these people make in this beautiful region of ours. And if you happen to pass by the !Khwa ttu San Culture and Education Centre, do pop in for coffee and cheesecake, and to browse around their interesting museum.

I have chosen some wines to go with a few favourite dishes – but remember there are no hard and fast rules. You choose, Skattie, as it is a very personal matter and each person should develop his or her own taste – although nothing can beat the classic combinations, such as a good Cabernet Sauvignon with my hearty oxtail stew! (p. 157)

Below are some tips.'

Tannie's Tips

Fish–Kabeljou, etc
Sauvignon Blanc
TRY ALSO
Blanc de Noir,
very light blends
of Red wine

Seafood–
mussels, prawns,
Crayfish –
Dry or off-dry
white wines,
Sauvignon Blanc,
Blanc de Blanc

Fish appetisers –
Dry Sparkling
white or rosé.

CURRIES
Fruity White,
Chenin Blanc

Chicken or Fish
in cream sauce –
Chardonnay

DESSERT
Sweet wines or
Demi-sec Sparkling

Roast Quail
Pinot, light reds
or light rosé

Hearty stews,
Rump, fillet steak
Cabernet Sauvignon

Guinea Fowl,
gamey dishes –
SHIRAZ

Roast chicken
Light reds or
white blends

PASTA
Good Red Quaffing

Watch a Show, Sithandwa!

From Icons and Aikonas

Me as Desmond Tutu

Me as that third-rate comedian that sometimes does me!

Talking kaktus with Jan van Riebeeck

Evita for president!

'Here are some snapshots of various performances we have given at the Perron. My favourite one is "Tannie Evita Praat Kaktus" (which sounds worse than it is!). It has been performed every Sunday since 1995 and adapts to the daily hiccups of politics. In it I take the acknowledged history of white South Africa and show you how politicians lied to us, brainwashed us while making themselves strong. Yes, let us remember where we come from, so we can truly celebrate where we are going! I also appear in various other entertainments, because what would the Perron be without its own Tannie Evita?

We also have a wonderful input from our local community. There is the old Baptikosweti Passport (from my Homeland Republic where I was the South African Ambassador during the 1980s. Or maybe you don't remember apartheid?) Anyone in the community can buy one for R20. I sign it like any other passport and then they can come and see any show at the Perron for R20, or "pay-what-you-can". That means we have been presented with bottles of home-made jam, olives, biltong, and even a small chicken. The chicken was called "Box Office" and eventually multiplied into a colony of small feathered chicks (until a stray dog ate them all on a Saturday afternoon when the Springboks lost to the All Blacks!)

So "Meet me at the Perron" means: everyone is welcome. See you there.'

Amandla Vrystaat!

'A few years ago, before the Polokwane Rubicon, it was my delight and honour to be the MC at former President FW de Klerk's 70th birthday dinner at the Mount Nelson (Mandela) Hotel in Cape Town.

A night to remember. I planned six costume changes, because I know how people look at what I wear. I remember dear little Princess Diana giving me that tip, and how she added to every now and then wear something really old to confuse all the experts. Well, I did: I wore Chris Levin (old), Errol Arendz (new), Francois Vedemme (new), Marianne Fassler (very new) and my son De Kock's friend Moff de Bruyn's latest creation. Unfortunately that zip broke when I hugged Madiba and so I couldn't turn my back on anyone all the time while wearing it.

FW was a delightful host and Elita the perfect hostess. People often mix us up, because of our names. What a V instead of an L can do! And then the guest list: Our generous Nelson Mandela, elegant Zanele Mbeki. There was legendary Helen Suzman, Prince Mangosutho Buthelezi, dierbare Archbishop Desmond Tutu (who always calls me "Ousie").

The night was a protocol nightmare. So I started: "Good evening," (in many languages, including Serbian, as the Crown Prince and Princess of Yugoslavia were special guests. How would I tell them that their country no longer existed?) "My name is Evita Bezuidenhout and I have been an icon (if not an aikona in today's politically correct structures) since 1978. I was a force to be reckoned with when FW de Klerk was just an ordinary Cabinet Minister, Mangosutho Buthelezi was known as Gatsha and wouldn't accept homeland status, but cashed the cheque. When Nelson Mandela was in jail and so banned we didn't even know what he looked like. When Thabo Mbeki was in exile, sipping whisky in a Swedish hotel paid for by the Anti-Apartheid Movement. When Helen Suzman was a leftwing irritation in our rightwing Parliament. And when Elita de Klerk was a sweet teenage girl on a sunny Greek beach. So let's leave protocol out tonight." Everyone was as relieved as I was. I allowed the lights to make my diamonds glitter, opened my arms and smiled. "As me, I welcome you and focus on him." And so I handed the mess over to FW. He rose to the occasion and it was a great success.

But it was more than just a birthday party. It was proof that we in South Africa didn't follow any blueprint; we *are* the blueprint! There sat former enemies, now friends. Former warriors, now just worriers. Former rivals, now retirees – and all proud South Africans. Yes, the square peg had found the round hole. The future was certain. It was just the past that was unpredictable.

As the past I knew what to say.

"Amandla Vrystaat!"

And that said it all.'

Ford Fairlane

TP 4501

This Ford Fairlane once belonged to Mrs Evita Bezuidenhout's husband, Oom Hasie. In 1958, Dr JJ de V Bezuidenhout became a cabinet minister in the government of Hendrik Verwoerd. The two bullet holes in the front window are a reminder of the failed assassination attempt on his life at the Wolwekloof turn-off along the Warmbad Road in 1959.

Dr Bezuidenhout was arrested in 1960 for breaking the Immorality Act. He was found on the backseat of this car in a compromising position with a Swazi waitress from the Laagerfontein Grand Hotel. After interventions by his wife and her powerful friends in the National Party, all charges against Minister Bezuidenhout were dropped. The woman disappeared.

Club Sandwiches

For one sandwich, remove the crusts from three large slices of bread. Spread butter on one side and place any two of these fillings on two of the slices. Put one slice on top of the other, filling side up, and cover with a third slice. Cut into quarters and cover with clingwrap until it's time to eat. Repeat with other fillings for a variety of sandwiches.

Merc

Cream cheese, cucumber slices, smoked salmon

Renault

Goat's cheese, black olive tapenade, lettuce

BMW

Pastrami, mustard, gherkins, lettuce

Lancia

Avocado slices, prawns, mayonnaise

Volvo

Herring strips, sliced beetroot, cream cheese

Alfa Romeo

Bean purée, Parma ham, black pepper

Peugeot

Roasted red peppers, slices of boiled egg, anchovies

Vauxhall

Crispy bacon, omelette

Backseat Buffet

Tannie Evita's diet

'There is always the morning after the night before – or the bathroom scale after the banquet. How many terrified moments have we not spent on the edge of that familiar hell, watching the dial creep up and over that minefield of fat? While compiling the cookbook, Linda and I were very aware that once you came to this page, you would already be wondering how you'd ever get back to what you weighed on page one.

Here's my solution: Tannie Evita's diet.'

You are what you eat...?

1. Confront your weight with energy and celebration. After all, what you now weigh is what you recently enjoyed!

2. I usually start my regime with a session at the Hydro in Stellenbosch (www.thehydro.co.za). They have a special deal that takes you from a Sunday afternoon till 11:00 on the next Wednesday. Book two consecutive weeks, which then gives you parole from the Wednesday afternoon till the next Sunday midday at home in real life. If you can keep up the regime of discipline while you're at home between Hydro sessions, you will lose weight there too.

3. The regime at the Hydro is fruit and salads. There are many choices. You don't have to starve. But you can rest and so stick to a fruit diet throughout with a salad dinner on the Tuesday evening before you leave.

4. Then let your own regime take over: cut down on wheat, dairy and sugar.

5. Don't punish yourself. Bit by bit you can conquer the mountain and turn it into a molehill. What I did is, once I came down from 98 kilos to 88 kilos, I bought 10 kilos of flour and kept it in the supermarket bag. Every time I was tempted to eat a chocolate or worse, I'd pick up the bag. That weight once lived on my body? Believe me, you will not want it back. You will not have that chocolate.

6. I am now between 80 and 83 kilos. My clothes fit, my energy has doubled, my appetite is controlled and my days start with a good laugh. Yes, start every day by standing in front of your full-length mirror naked. And laugh!

The Ultimate recipe for Reconciliation

'I have said: to eat with friends is to renew friendship, to further embrace friends and create new lasting relationships. Now imagine, if you put enemies around a table, what can they do but talk? They can't fight: too many knives and forks. Serve them a plate of your favourite food and watch enemies realise that they love the same thing. Why should they fight? Let them celebrate their passion and make peace.

All good and well.

I sent my recipe for bobotie to The Troubles in Northern Ireland and it worked. I sent it to North and South Korea and they're now eating it with chopsticks and Geiger counters. North Korea keeps firing missiles, but I see that as them celebrating their enjoyment of my bobotie. I even sent that recipe to the Congo Peace Accord with our former Minister of Foreign Affairs, Nkosazana Dlamini-Zuma, but then she ate the recipe.

But reconciliation can also start at home. A percentage of the sales of this cookbook goes to The Darling Trust. It started at Evita se Perron in Darling as an outreach programme for the cultural upliftment of the community, with the Elsie Balt Art School, a piano school, reading sessions and quarterly talent shows. But soon it became urgent to structure our commitment into a trust, and today we thank many people in South Africa and overseas for their financial assistance and donations. Thank you for buying this cookbook. Buy another one for an English friend and one also for an Afrikaanse maatjie. Soon we will be available in Dutch and German. This recipe for reconciliation is very simple. Look around and listen. Who needs to feel important? Who is lonely? Who is frightened? Who is new in the neighbourhood? Who lives next door? Take them some koeksisters, invite them to tea and melktert, take their children to the seaside or the opera. Or a hip-hop rave! Talk. Share. Recognise optimism and believe that for every piece of bad news, there are three pieces of good news. Look for them and find them. And pass them on. And if you bake your cakes and sell them on a Saturday morning at the village market, deposit that money in The Darling Trust account and let us know. You will be surprised how much happiness can come from the smallest gift.'

Acknowledgements

'To all the people who gave the recipes and who have shared my table over the past 50 years.

Seasoning is a great art. When I ask for a recipe of a dish that I enjoyed, the good cook normally just says – "a little bit of this, a little bit of that ..." So I find giving exact measurements very difficult. It takes experience to know just the right amount of herbs and spices to add to a dish, so carry on cooking and experimenting.

Good dinners make happy people!'

The Darling Trust

The Darling Trust was established in August 2003 by founding member and now trustee, Pieter-Dirk Uys, and is structured to focus on three areas:

- arts, culture and customs
- community needs through education
- health and environment, with the accent on HIV/AIDS.

The vision of the Trust is to:

- manage funds through an informed, researched and transparent structure
- create a blueprint for other smaller communities
- keep our people healthy through education and care
- empower people through developing talents and skills
- assist our communities with the challenges of HIV/AIDS.

The Darling Trust is there to support the community of Darling, who have adopted me as their Fairy Gogo-mama! A plate of bobotie doesn't solve everything. Money can. Visit www.thedarlingtrust.org.

Glossary

Methods

al dente – firm enough to bite into

baste – pouring or brushing fat, juices or marinade over food while cooking

braai – an emotional word in South Africa. It entails far more than standing around a fire grilling meat. Can only be understood once personally experienced. See also 'potjiekos' and 'skottelbraai'

braise – frying food lightly and then stewing slowly in a covered cooking vessel

caramelise – heating sugar or syrup until it turns brown and thickish

sauté – quick-frying food in shallow oil

smoor – slowly cooking over low heat in a covered vessel, usually with onions, potatoes, and a little fat and liquid

skottelbraai – stir-frying in a wok over gas or coals – outside. Closely associated with braai

Ingredients and recipes

atjar – mixture of finely chopped vegetables and fruit marinated in vinegar, eaten as a relish with meat

baguette – French loaf

biryani – a rice-based meal made with spices, rice (usually basmati) and meat, chicken or vegetables

blini – a thin Russian pancake, similar to a crêpe; the main difference between the two is that yeast may be used in blinis, but not in crêpes

boeremeisies – apricots marinated in brandy

boerewors – South African braai sausage. See 'braai'

borscht – a soup popular in many Eastern European countries. The main ingredient is beetroot, which gives it a deep reddish-purple colour

bredie – the South African equivalent for stew

bruschetta – grilled bread rubbed with garlic and topped with extra-virgin olive oil, salt and pepper

cassoulet – a rich, slow-cooked bean stew or casserole originating in the south of France, containing meat (typically pork sausages, pork, goose, duck and sometimes mutton), pork skin (couennes) and white haricot beans

clafoutis – a French dessert made by baking fresh fruit (traditionally cherries) and a batter resembling a combination of Yorkshire pudding batter and custard

crème fraîche – a soured cream containing about 28% butterfat, soured with bacterial culture; it is less sour than sour cream, but thicker in consistency

crudité – mixed raw vegetables to dip in a sauce

dukkah – an Indian mix of dried nuts, spices, salt and pepper, to eat with bread and crackers

fricassee – meat cooked in a white wine sauce

frikkadel – South African meatball

frittata – the Italian version of an omelette, made with vegetables

garlic yogurt – plain Bulgarian yoghurt mixed with fresh, crushed garlic and a pinch of salt

gratin – a culinary technique by which an ingredient is topped with a browned crust consisting of breadcrumbs, grated cheese, egg and/or butter

hummus – paste made from ground chickpeas and sesame seeds, eaten as a dip

kofta – a Middle Eastern and South Asian meatball or dumpling usually made with beef or lamb and mixed with spices and onions

koeksisters – South African confection consisting of plaited dough strips deep-fried in oil and then dipped in a sweet syrup

kolwyntjies – small cakes decorated with icing sugar

latke – potato pancakes

malva pudding – spongy pudding named after the Afrikaans word for marshmallows

melktert – another South African delicacy – a crusty tart with a filling consisting mostly of milk, sugar and eggs, and sprinkled with cinnamon

pampoenkoekies – South African pumpkin fritters

peperonata – a dish made with stewed peppers

pilaf – a rice dish cooked with meat and spices

potjiekos – another emotionally charged South African way of cooking bredie in a traditional three-legged black pot on hot coals

purée – pulped fruit or vegetables

puri – an Asian unleavened bread

putupap – porridge cooked dry and eaten with tomato relish and braaivleis

ragout – a thick, hearty stew of French origin

rösti – a Swiss dish made with grated potatoes mixed with some butter or fat and salt and pepper, and fried

sambal – relish made with vegetables or fruit and spices

skordalia – garlic dip of Greek origin

sosaties – the South African version of kebabs

stroganoff – a Russian dish of sautéed beef strips served in a sauce with sour cream

tzatziki – a Greek meze, also used as a sauce for souvlaki and gyros

umngqusho – samp and beans, a favourite South African staple food

vetkoek – small bread bun made of light dough and deep-fried in oil

vichyssoise – a French-style soup made of puréed leeks, onions, potatoes, cream, and chicken stock, which is traditionally served cold

vinaigrette – a mixture of vinegar, oil, herbs and spices used as salad dressing

waterblommetjies – a water plant with fragrant white flowers, found in the Western Cape and used for a traditional South African bredie

zucchini – courgettes – small vegetable marrows

Register

appetisers and snacks
antipasto 64
apéritif snacks 18
'caviar' butter appetiser 50
cheese toasts 18
chilli bites 29
cucumber rounds 19
dukkah 41
hot cashew nuts 18
marrow bones on toast 62
Parmesan toasts 15
pear mice meeting 35
the Perron snackplatter 105

beans
bush cassoulet 44
butter bean purée 75
butter beans and tuna 99
green bean bredie 25
heerenbone 33
heerenbone with onions 33
samp and beans 89

beef
beef stroganoff 51
beef with pearl onions 25
meatballs 69
mincemeat with peas 41
oxtail stew 57
steak kebabs 92
whole beef fillet 55

bobotie
Bambi bobotie 75 .
bobotie squares 18
reconciliation bobotie 53

bread
cinnamon toast 99
Evita's home-baked bread 105
herb toast 99
Jean's mieliebread 80
puri 43
roosterkoek 92
vetkoek 93

bredies, stews, and potjiekos
cumin chicken with sweet
   potatoes 25
curry potjie 97
green bean bredie 25
lamb casserole 33
Oom Rudolf's potjie 97
oxtail stew 57
pumpkin bredie 31
ultimate tomato bredie 97
Winnie's Stompie ragout 111

cakes and tarts
apple tart 80
apricot tart 39
cheesecake 84
crunchy chocolate cake 71
Ouma Ossewania's brandewynkoek 106
Tannie's melktert 107
Uda's orange cake 85
yoghurt cake 85

chicken
chicken balls 18, 79
chicken curry 31
chicken kebabs 27, 92
chicken liver and onions 66
chicken liver sosaties 92
chicken peri-peri 60
chicken satays 19
chicken soup and stock 11
chicken with nuts 95
chopped liver 49
cumin chicken with sweet potatoes 25
Darling chicken pie 77
ginger chicken stir-fry 79
Hungarian chicken 49
Moroccan chicken 73
noodle stir-fry 95
roast chicken 55
Shabir's gold coin fricassee 110

couscous
couscous 73
roast sweet potato and couscous 21

curry
chicken curry 31
curry potjie 97
fish curry 28
potato and pea curry 43
Thai green curry 71

desserts
baked apple clowns 35
caramelised oranges 51
clafoutis 99
Evita's malva pudding 80
figs and mozzarella 66
fresh and dried fruit kebabs 35
koeksisters 53
Koornhof's Cape Coloured surprise 115
Laagerfontein Hotel mess 115
orange ambrosia 31
orange trifle 81
raspberry coulis 115
raspberry fool 115
strawberry delight 73
stuffed peaches 67
walnut balls 29

dips, sauces, and oils
apple chutney 101
blatjang 101
chilli herb oil 101
courgette dip 70
hummus 99
shrimp dip 72
skordalia 68
sweet chilli dipping sauce 71
tomato sauce 64, 69
tzatziki 68
waterblommetjie mousse 15
yoghurt relish 40

eggs and omelettes
asparagus omelette 16
spicy vinegar eggs 41
stuffed eggs 18
vegetable frittata 65

fish and seafood
crayfish 94
fish curry 28
fish rissoles 28
harders 94
hot garlic prawns 60
kingklip kebabs 94
periwinkles 37
pickled fish 31
prawn kebabs 19
salmon fillet 62
salmon tartare 62
sea urchins 37
smoorsnoek 28
toasted sardines 99
whole Cape salmon 59
whole kabeljou 94

gratins
courgette gratin 61
fennel gratin 61
onion gratin 61
potato gratin 61
putupap gratin 87

guinea fowl
guinea fowl in red wine 56
guinea fowl with sultanas and hanepoot 56

jam
apricot jam 101

Register

Published in 2010 by Umuzi
an imprint of Random House
Struik (Pty) Ltd
Company Reg No
1966/003153/07
80 McKenzie Street, Cape Town
8001, South Africa
PO Box 1144, Cape Town 8000,
South Africa
umuzi@randomstruik.co.za
www.umuzi-randomhouse.co.za

First edition, first printing 2010
10 9 8 7 6 5 4 3 2 1

ISBN 978-1-4152-0090-2

Original design by
Linda Vicquery.
Cover design and layout
by mr design.
Cover photography by
Kelly Walsh.
Photographer's assistant:
Rhonda Millard.
Stylist: Chris Koch.
Additional props:
Frits van Ryneveld of
Mantis Trading Store.
Set in Corporate.
Printed and bound by Tien Wah
Press, Singapore.

Photographs by Crispian Plunkett
(p.2), Diana Ginsberg (p.4), Lionel Friedberg (pp.5, 65), Pat Bromilow-Downing (pp.6, 13, 14, 17, 19, 23, 24, 29, 34, 45, 67, 69, 70, 78, 80, 81, 89, 90, 97, 106, 128), Ruphin Coudyzer (pp.8, 100), Brent Meersman (p.10), Mark Staines (p.11), Anton Geldenhuys (pp.50, 85, 98), Daron Chatz (p.63), Richard Cuttler, 1985 (p.74), Benny Gool, 1994 (pp.83), Liezel van der Merwe (pp.105, 107, 108, 120), Kelly Walsh (p.109, 111), Marius Roux (p.116), and Dirk Visser (p.119).

Paintings of Evita in the style of the masters by Nina van der Westhuizen are: *Self-Portrait* by Frida Kahlo, 1940 (p.26), *Berber Girl* by Irma Stern, 1945 (p.30), *A Bust of a Young Woman Smiling* by Rembrandt van Rijn, 1633 (p.33), *Seated Woman (Marie-Thérèse)* by Pablo Picasso, 1937 (p.38), imitating *Marilyn Monroe* by Andy Warhol (p.43), *Madonna and Child* by Carlos Crivelli, 1490 (p.46), *Portrait of Ira P* by Tamara de Lempicka, 1930 (p.48), *Fruits of Bali* by Vladimir Tretchikoff, ca 1950 (p.52), *Portrait of Adele Bloch-Bauer I* by Gustav Klimt, 1907 (p.57), *The Clothed Maja* by Francisco Goya, ca 1803 (p.72), *Madonna del Granduca* by Raphael, 1505 (p.76), *Woman with Plants* by Grant Wood, 1929 (p.101), *Mona Lisa* by Leonardo da Vinci, 1503 (p.102), *The Girl with the Pearl Earring* by Johannes Vermeer, ca 1665 (p.117), *Liberty Leading the People* by Eugène Delacroix, 1830 (p.123).

Other paintings are the still life with pomegranates, 2000 (p.20) and *Marigolds in Karen's Vase* (p.40) by Elmie Smit-Erasmus, *Still life with Dasseneiland* (p.36) by Nina van der Westhuizen, and a detail from a painting by Nicholas de Klerk, 1983 (p.110).